wish you were here

WISH YOU WERE HERE

TRAVELS THROUGH LOSS AND HOPE

AMY WELBORN

IMAGE BOOKS·NEW YORK

IMAGE

Library of Congress Cataloging-in-Publication Data
Welborn, Amy.
Wish you were here: travels through loss and hope /
Amy Welborn. — 1st ed.
        p.   cm.
1. Welborn, Amy—Travel—Italy—Sicily. 2. Sicily (Italy)—Description and
travel. 3. Widows—Biography. 4. Catholics—Biography. I. Title.
BX4705.W4515A3 2012
282.092—dc23
        [B]   2011017119

ISBN 978-0-307-71638-5
eISBN 978-0-307-71639-2

Printed in the United States of America

Book design by Lauren Dong
Cover design by Erin Schell
Cover photography © Gary S. Chapman/Getty Images

1 3 5 7 9 10 8 6 4 2

First Edition

To belong to him, to be called by him, is to be rooted in life indestructible.

—JOSEPH RATZINGER, *Eschatology*

WISH YOU WERE HERE

Introduction

I RACED INTO THE BACKYARD JUST AFTER MIDNIGHT. Barefoot, in pajamas, I raised an empty brown pill bottle into the frigid Kansas darkness, swept it through the air, snapped the white disc of a lid on top, and then rushed back into the silent house, through the hall into my room, wrote on a slip of paper, and taped it to the bottle.

Air—the label said—*from 1970*.

The bottle still rattles around in a drawer in my father's house, I think. I wouldn't throw it away if I ran across it. I wouldn't open it either. I don't know why. After all, it's only air.

~

Here's what I remember from the first days of a February years later.

Sunday morning, we arrived at Mass at Our Lady of Sorrows parish so late that the only seats left were in the balcony. The first scripture reading was already happening by the time the five of us squeezed into the pew: me; my husband, Mike; our two little boys, Joseph and Michael; and Katie, my teenaged daughter from my first marriage.

The elderly pastor—elfin in appearance, but resonant and dramatic in tone, always ending his sentences with a forceful, downward emphasis as if his words were screws he was forcing into a particularly tough board—began to preach from the sanctuary below us. In the Gospel that morning, Jesus had exorcised demons, but this would not be Monsignor's subject. That would be death, of course.

Mike and I glanced at each other, amused. For in the five months we had attended Mass in the parish in our new city of Birmingham, Alabama, we'd noticed this about the pastor: he liked to talk about death. No matter what the Gospel or the feast, it seemed, he'd find his way to it: we are all going to die and there is no more important task than preparing for the certainty. No surprise, really. The man had spent his adult life ministering to the dying and the grieving, and he was in his late seventies himself. Death might be on his mind.

So that morning, nodding only briefly to Jesus and the demons, Monsignor moved on to a book he'd been given about life-after-death experiences, and here we were again at death's door, where he would talk to us about death and—always his most repeated point—being prepared for it.

So yes, I remember glancing at Mike and him glancing back and I remember sharing knowing, slight smiles at death's introduction. And we settled back to listen, to pray, to think about work tomorrow, about the next book or article deadline, all of us up there in the balcony, an enormous bas-relief of that Lady of Sorrows cradling her dead son on the sanctuary wall behind the altar straight ahead of us, in plain view.

I remember Mike kneeling beside me after Communion. I remember because his posture was just a little different than normal. He usually looked ahead, or down at a misbehaving son, or just rested his chin on his folded hands. That morning, I remember, he knelt there, his face buried in his hands.

I remember that we went to Whole Foods after Mass and the boys picked out muffins and Katie got a croissant and Mike wandered off to look for something and he came back with a bag of loose tea because that was his latest thing. He said this was part

of his renewed project of getting back into shape, a project interrupted by our move and the substantial pressures of his new job
as director of evangelization (and the Pro-Life Office . . . and
the Family Life Office . . . and the Campus Ministry Office . . .
and the Child Protection Office . . . he seemed to add a job every
month we'd lived there) for the diocese. Mike was a man of rou-
tines, and this transition had messed with his running and lifting
schedule in a big way. He wasn't in the worst shape he'd ever been
but neither was he in the best, so in this new year, he'd get back
on track.

For some reason, the tea would evidently be a part of that. I
remember him walking down the aisle, cradling boxes of tea and
a box of filters in his arms. The tea was green, because cutting
down on caffeine would be part of the renewed health regime too.

And I remember him wrapping his arms around me at the
Botanical Gardens a few hours later.

It was February, and although a few weeks later it would snow,
that day it was mild enough for a walk in and through the various, quite diverse areas of that beautiful public space: the Japanese garden, hills rich with ferns, the greenhouse desert—all of
us except Katie, who stayed back at the apartment, swamped with
homework.

I remember how when we had arrived and I was getting ready
to close up and lock the car, I held my camera in my hand and
debated whether I should bring it along or not.

I looked around at the still mostly dead, not quite budding
vegetation. I considered the boys and Mike waiting for me near
the fountain at the entrance. No, I decided. There will be another
time—later, when there's more in bloom and more color. We'll all
come back then and there will be more pictures.

Yes, I remember how Mike grabbed me and hugged me in the
middle of the Alabama Woodlands, boys tramping through the
dry brown leaves thick across the ground around us. I remember
how happy we were—ecstatic, even—to be back in the South,

to never have to endure another northern Indiana winter, those months of backbreaking snow that just seemed to go on and on. Not here. Very soon, the dogwoods would be budding, the pink and violet azaleas would be blossoming, and we would return to walk in the gardens again, to see the colors, to relax in the certainty of new life gently but surely overwhelming the old. It would all happen, we were certain: another walk, another spring. Years of them, stretching ahead.

I remember the next evening, which was February 2, the Feast of the Presentation, a celebration of the day Joseph and Mary took the baby Jesus to the Temple forty days after his birth as a symbolic offering of their child to God. I decided we would do a special prayer before dinner, so I printed out a very condensed version of Night Prayer: the last of the daily prayers in the Liturgy of the Hours. Now, that Night Prayer, or Compline, always includes a prayer called the Nunc Dimittis, words taken directly from the Gospel of Luke. An elderly man named Simeon met the Holy Family at the Temple that day and thanked God in words very appropriate for those minutes before we release ourselves to sleep:

> *Now, Master, you may let your servant go in peace, according to your word,*
> *for my eyes have seen your salvation, which you prepared in sight of all the peoples,*
> *a light for revelation to the Gentiles, and glory for your people Israel.*

Those of us who could read, recited it aloud; those of us who couldn't, fidgeted. Mike knew it by heart because he prayed these prayers every day himself, and had almost his whole adult life, as a seminarian, as a Catholic priest, and after leaving active priestly ministry in 1993, as a layman working in education and Catholic publishing. He never stopped praying those prayers. I remember that deep voice. I can hear it now.

Lord, now you may let your servant go in peace . . .

I remember him sitting on the couch after dinner, laughing at a sitcom. I remember him raising himself grudgingly from that couch to head trudging, so tired, into our room, where his computer waited for him, and where he needed to finish up his column for the diocesan newspaper, due tomorrow. He had been so tired so early in the evenings for the past couple of months, so tired so early at night, it sometimes seemed as if he wouldn't make it down that short hall from the living room to the bedroom. But, he had been saying, getting into shape would take care of it. He would get his energy back.

Still thinking about that column, he posted on Facebook in the early evening. Eventually, he got it done, that column. He wrote things in it like, "None of us knows what the future holds," and, quoting his friend Fr. Benedict Groeschel, "We have no plans except to be led by God."

That's what the man wrote.

I remember.

If I could put it all in a bottle, snap the lid on tight, and keep it forever, I would. But this—this is the best I can do.

~

The next afternoon—it was a Tuesday—I slumped against the cool tiled wall of a hospital emergency room, looking at him for the first time since he and Joseph had left the apartment earlier that morning.

He was covered with a light blue sheet up to his bare shoulders; he looked as if he were dozing on the table on the other side of the room.

But he was dead.

He had been dead all day, and I didn't even know it.

⁓

They had left the apartment that morning, he and seven-year-old Joseph, just as they always did, around 7:30. He'd dropped Joseph off at school, then driven directly to the YMCA down the road. He'd just started going there; they didn't know him at the front desk yet, couldn't tell you who he was. He went to the locker room, changed his clothes, stepped on a treadmill, and started to run.

After about ten minutes, he raised the speed. I know this because the woman running next to him noticed, impressed because he was holding that quicker pace.

Then he dropped to the floor, hard. She was a dentist and had CPR training, so she knew what to do and what to look for. "His eyes were open," she told me kindly but bluntly over the phone two weeks later, "but there was nothing there."

I was grateful to her. But I was also jealous. Resentful, even. She'd been with him when my husband, my best friend, drew his last breath.

Not me.

So what was I doing while my husband died? Mundane things, the things I did most every day. I had basically spent the morning blogging about churchy matters, throwing some laundry into the wash, reading to four-year-old Michael, and being irritated about the inevitability of dinner. I was at a point of great frustration with everyone's varied culinary and dietary needs and desires—a daughter convinced she was fat but who wouldn't eat fresh vegetables, a husband who only wanted to eat fresh vegetables, and two little boys who really wouldn't eat anything that didn't lie on the color spectrum from beige to brown. Yes, having to deal with dinner for this picky crowd struck me as a big problem, an obstacle to my complete happiness.

The phone call came at one, just as Michael had gone for his nap on his lower bunk in the boys' room. The caller ID screen on the phone in the kitchen identified the source of the call as a local hospital, and I almost didn't answer it, assuming it was a wrong number. But I did and I listened in growing confusion as the woman on the other end asked if my name was Amy. After I said yes, she told me that there was someone named Mike at the hospital there who was associated with someone named Amy and they wondered if I was the Amy in question so would I please come down so they could check it out. Seriously. That was all I could get out of the woman except the advice to leave my young child at home. They wouldn't even answer my direct questions. "Is it 'Dubruiel'? Is he alive?"

"Please just come down. Ask for Lee. Do you know where to park?"

So over the course of a hideous forty-five minutes, I put Michael in the car, trying not to wake him, drove to Katie's school, got her out of class, and drove back to the apartment, where she would stay with him. On the drive, I whispered a report of the phone call, telling her and telling myself that even if something had happened to Mike, he was probably still alive. Surely. We told ourselves that. But even as I assured her, I was shaking, inside and out.

On the way downtown by myself, I prayed and cried hard. I banged the steering wheel and shook it; I told myself, *He's alive, he's alive, he's alive* . . . I tried to tell God—I shouted at God—to make sure he remembered, we just moved here . . . *he's only fifty . . . two little boys . . .*

. . . *he's alive, he's alive.*

Please.

❧

It's late June now, almost five months after that day, and the four of us, Katie, the two little boys, and I—without a drop of Italian blood between us—are hauling suitcases over cobblestones in a tiny little town in the north of Sicily. We make a ridiculous, embarrassing amount of noise as we bump our way through a small plaza past a small fountain, headed to one of the three streets in this tiny, quiet village.

I had parked the compact white rental car in the lot outside the village, only understanding later, in retrospect, what the elderly lot attendant had been trying to tell me, in his mix of Italian and English—that although cars were prohibited in the village, generally, it would be perfectly all right for me to pull up to the door of the B and B and unload.

But I didn't understand, and I see him shake his head at us as we walk away, clattering. Except for all our commotion, the street—which seems to be the only real street in the village—is empty. We pass a large stone fountain in the middle of the tiny square, pouring out fresh *acqua* from its spout. We keep walking, suitcase wheels taking a beating, past a vending machine that sells contact lenses, past the parish church, past white plastic tables and chairs in a shaded courtyard, and finally arrive at the *pensione* where we would spend the next few days of summer.

Just down the hill, a half mile away, the Mediterranean glistened, a brilliant blue. We drove along it on our way here from the Palermo airport, and we would step into its waters several times over the next two weeks to let ourselves be cooled by the sea. We would wade in it and plunge into it here in the north, and a week later, far on the other side, the southern coast of Sicily. In between, we would see ruins and castles, we'd get lost, eat gelato, light candles in dark churches, and pray under stars. And every moment of it, I would look for him.

It was like that every day at home, anyway, so why not? Why not take that daily routine of remembering and searching, of excavation of life and death, those memories of my husband laughing, of his body cooling under a blue sheet, that constant deep, frantic prayer for his little boys, why not take the cross and the empty tomb, weeping mothers and wounds probed by a doubter—why not take it all out of a beige-colored third-floor apartment in an

Alabama summer, heavy with humidity, memories, and land-marks, why not wrest the top off the bottle of the past and spill it out here?

In the pictures in the guidebooks to Sicily, all I saw was the past, remnants of what was dead and gone. It seemed right. Maybe here in Sicily, picking my way on worn-down paths around tum-bling ancient walls and broken columns, I will catch a clue as to how to live with it all. And because here the veil between past and present seems as thin as the cooling breeze from the sea, maybe, just once in a while, it will whip aside, it will lift, and I'll see.

❦

This book is about how we got from here to there, from February to June, from Alabama to Sicily, and why. It's not my autobiogra-phy or his biography or a portrait of our marriage. It's not a theo-logical treatise on the Last Things—far from it—or a guide on how to live with grief. It's a memoir of what we—mostly I—went through, thought, prayed, and did during a trip to Sicily, a place I had never once before thought about going in forty-nine years of life, a trip I impulsively planned about a month after my husband died of a heart attack.

I wrote it because, as a longtime book, column, and blog writer about matters of faith and life, I could not avoid writing about grief and loss and faith in the months after Mike's death. I did wait, though. I hesitated every time before tapping the "pub-lish" button on my blog because I didn't want to be seen as seek-ing sympathy or exploiting it. Exploiting him.

But then every time I would go ahead and post a blog entry related to grief, readers' reactions—as they thanked me and, most helpfully, shared their own experiences—convinced me it might be all right.

There was something else, too.

People kept dying. They just wouldn't stop.

The mother of one of my daughter's classmates, a woman

younger than I am, dropped dead of an aneurysm. Two weeks later, another classmate of Katie's died in a car accident.

An online friend of mine, a fellow writer nicknamed the "Internet Monk," Michael Spencer, was diagnosed with cancer in the late fall and died the day after Easter, aged fifty-two.

The fall after Mike died, in fact, eight months to the day, on October 3, my good friend Molly, who lived in Florida, died. She had taught my children, I hers, and she had been battling various forms of cancer for years. That evening, one of her daughters wrote, she "went peacefully home."

If we are Christians, we have two kinds of hope constantly held out to us: the hope that the cross gives, that our sins have no more power over us, that in our suffering we are not alone, that God knows, that God suffers, mysteriously with us; and the hope of the empty tomb, that death has no more power over us either, that Jesus Christ lives.

But still, in the midst of the hope, the pietà remains. There is Our Lady of Sorrows, there is the mother standing at the cross, weeping, there are the friends, uncomprehending and regretful, there is a suddenly empty space and strange silence, there are the doubters scoffing from afar, challenging, *Where is your hope now?*

So we went to Sicily, to see.

1

I SEE DADDY'S PLANE!
If you heard a four-year-old yelping these words at the airport gate, you'd probably think nothing of it except to pray the clearly excitable boy was not on your flight and please, God, not in your row.

Me, I'm no stranger to the boy. He's one of mine, and he will definitely be on my flight, in my row, probably on my lap for most of this day and the next. Here in the Birmingham airport, he's standing at the window of glass across the waiting area, pointing it out:

Daddy's plane!

My heart skips, my insides knot up tightly, as they still do at every mention, every thought of him: *DaddyMichaelMike*. My soul takes the quick but familiar tumble down the steps of past and present reality: *LoveMissGone*.

I zip up the emotions, the desire to just stand up and do my own shouting—*Why?* I pack it away like I'd crammed all the clothes I'd need for the next three weeks in the single suitcase at my feet, and I look around. Michael's over there yelling about his father, but he's doing it cheerfully, so I'm not really worried about him—puzzled, maybe, but not worried. He's a good-natured four-year-old, likes Batman well enough, but Spider-Man more, and talks easily about his father, gone almost five months now. He has only cried once. It was in late March, about two months after the day his father died.

"Can God get Daddy out of heaven?"

"Why?"

"Because I want Daddy to be with us."

"He's happy. He's with God. He's the happiest, like we'll be when we go to heaven."

I was sitting on the bottom bunk with him, saying words like that, trying to believe them myself. Joseph, now eight years old, was on his way up to the top bunk. He paused on the ladder. All I could see were his feet. He stood there, silent, as his little brother tearfully argued his case:

"But I don't want Daddy to be invisible."

All we knew in those early days was absence. Empty space. Silence. Gone. No good-bye. Usually when Michael brings up his father, Joseph covers his ears and shakes his head back and forth, back and forth. "Don't talk about Daddy," he says if he can manage to say anything at all. "It makes me feel sad."

And sometimes Joseph just sits or lies down and cries through the litany of this long season: "IwantDaddyIwantDaddyIwant Daddy."

Me too.

When he censors himself and doesn't allow himself to speak for fear of the tears, he will still hug and be hugged, though. He won't resist, unless you try to make him talk. That's the way it was that night. Joseph came willingly from his own room into ours—mine now—and he sat on my lap for a while. We didn't say anything, we just sat there, rocking. Scattered on the walls, on the bookshelves, on Mike's desk were various icons, crucifixes, and other images—Jesus, Mary, St. Joseph, Padre Pio, Solanus Casey, Adam and Eve.

A photo collage of Mike and his boys on the dresser.

Visible. Every one of them.

～

"There's another one! There's two of Daddy's planes!"

As Michael presses his face against the floor-to-ceiling terminal window, Katie, seventeen, and I glance at each other and then both look around, thinking the same thing. Where's Joseph?

For he's the one I worry about the most. He's the one who would be startled and then elated by a flash of possibility that Daddy *could actually be on a plane*, right here with us, and then crushed by the now familiar, but still strange tumble down the steps of reality:

Love.

　　Miss.

　　　　Gone.

Katie knows this and as we look around, for a brief moment just a little panicked, we see that he's safe from false hopes this time. He's on the other side of the waiting area, absorbed in a video game over in a corner where he's found an outlet to recharge. I'm usually the pop-culture Taliban with the kids, but I've let him hang out in the Pokémon universe without many limits over the past few months. It's a complex world, this Pokémon world where a myriad of strange creatures with different types of power fight. It engages his gift for planning and lets him do battle. He needs to do battle, for he is feeling at war with what life and its companion death have brought him. Let the boy battle bad guys, safely. Let him figure things out, let him find paths to safety, even if it's only on a screen. So the little machine has been broken out for the journey, for the twenty-four hours of travel ahead, from Alabama to Sicily, via Charlotte, New York, Barcelona, and Milan.

Wait. What? How many hours? What was I thinking?

Well, too late for doubts. Here we are, ready to take off. Back to the four-year-old in the present, at the window, pointing.

What is he thinking?

Maybe that since he's told heaven is "up" and flying is the only way up for him right now, across the sea to wherever Mommy is taking him, it must be so for Daddy, too? Is he thinking that this is the plane Daddy rode to heaven?

I think of other planes as I wonder what he might mean. Planes of existence, mostly, for they obsess me these days.

Grief means sadness, of course. I would have expected that. But what I wouldn't have anticipated—if I were anticipating my husband's death, which of course, I wasn't—is this other thing, the thing that haunts as strongly as the sadness, sometimes more so: a strange, confusing, and constant feeling of dislocation and imbalance. He was just here a minute ago. He just can't not be here, just like that, can he?

I stayed in a room with his body in his open casket for four hours at his wake; I sang (grudgingly) *Alleluia* along with the rest of my fellow Christians weeks later at the end of that first Lent, feeling like an imposter as I did—but the question still hung, unanswered, and every journal entry from those first months ends the same way:

Where are you? Where did you go?

I searched for a while, tried to navigate those planes of existence, looking for a crack. I did so frantically at first, then, as the weeks went by, more methodically and even absently when I had a spare minute. Might as well look. Nothing better to do, nothing else to do but look for him, to solve this mystery.

I dug through his drawers, searched his pockets, went through the boxes of files and notebooks and pictures stacked in the closet in the apartment. I pored over the documents in his computer, read his e-mail. I have no idea what I was looking for. Nothing in particular, really. I didn't expect to hear his footstep or voice as I searched. I just hoped for a sign, I guess. A sign that it's all true, that it's real, those words I say in the Creed and have said all my life: *I believe in life everlasting.*

He must still *be*. Must be somewhere—there must be a plane where he exists, where he's still alive. God says so, right? Can I go there? Can I reach it? Can he reach me? Faith tells me that as gone as he is, there is really no such thing as *gone*; there's no permanent, definitive separation. Christ came to dwell in me when water was sprinkled on my forehead when I was a baby. I eat what looks like bread and drink what tastes like wine, but it's really God. There in those things I can see and touch—here, there, now, and forever meet. So maybe if I just keep digging, touching, staring at his handwriting in his planner, surely I'll reach him. Surely if I find the right object or concentrate hard enough, the planes can cross and I can know, and in some way, he'll be visible again.

Daddy's plane.

Then it comes to me. I don't have a precocious little mystic over there. Mike had luggage tags on his suitcases, and they were all Southwest Air. A row of bright blue and orange Southwest jets are lined up outside the window now. That's what the little boy saw, that's what reminded him of the tags, of the bags in his father's hands, sitting in the closet where I search.

He found him.

～

The first leg of the trip, from Birmingham to Charlotte, is delayed. We wait at the gate, we finally board, the male flight attendant crisply threatens to toss a persistently complaining passenger from the flight, it's forty-five minutes on, there are more problems, but finally we're on our way.

Both boys have flown before a few times, but neither remembers anything about the experiences a couple of years ago, flying from Indiana to Florida, Indiana to Arizona. They are both amazed as we rise up and the city shrinks below us and we cut through clouds. High clouds. Clouds close to heaven. Michael giggles. "I guess airplanes aren't bored," he says.

～

We are off, we are up. I finger the smooth cover of my bible. It's not a literal Word-of-God bible, but my own inspired scripture for this trip, many sheets of paper printed off from my computer and bound in a plastic folder—just the right one picked over and selected for its just-rightness at Staples. It's pretty shocking, actually. I've loved and coveted office supplies since I was a child, true, but lists and written plans—what you actually *use* the office supplies for—are things in life I rarely compose.

Ah, but wait a minute, sister—as my husband used to say—if you are hauling three kids to Europe for three weeks all by yourself, you might want to have a plan, might want to write a few things down.

Hence, the bible. Flight information, flight insurance, health insurance, accommodations information and maps (two bed and breakfasts and an *agriturismo* in Sicily, plus an apartment in Barcelona), copies of passports, rental car information, and emergency contact information. And on the front, slipped carefully into the clear plastic cover, photos printed out from the Internet of two landmarks: the Tonnara di Scopello in Sicily and Sagrada Família in Barcelona, with "Sicily & Barcelona, 2009" printed in picturesque, squiggly lettering. Veranda font, I believe. It's one of my favorites.

My bible was lovely. Is lovely, for I still have it, flip through it sometimes and imagine future journeys. On the actual trip I barely cracked it open. But the travel bible also carried a subtext.

Emergencies was the theme of the first page, a page filled with names of people and agencies and telephone numbers. The night before we left I sat down with my daughter and went through it with her. Text emerged from subtext.

"If something happens . . ."

"Nothing's going to . . ."

"If something happens, contact the consulate first, then Chris in Atlanta, then Grandfather, then the travel insurance company, then David in Rome . . ."

"Mom, nothing . . ."

"I could get hit by a bus. I could have a stroke. I could just collapse and die. It happens."

Silence fell between us, between my daughter and me.

"I know."

~

We've got an unbelievable itinerary in front of us for the next twenty-four hours—the price of scoring unbelievably cheap tickets being many transfers, in this case—and I can only just pray that everyone endures, including me. But I'm still relieved, for whatever lies ahead, I feel as I settle in my seat and slip the bible back into my bag, will be an improvement over what I left behind. I'm glad that for three weeks, I won't be sitting in our apartment—our temporary quarters until we sold the Indiana house and bought something new and great in Birmingham. The apartment was fine, but it didn't feel like home, and even less so without Mike. So yes, getting away from all of that is better.

Better than living above the elderly lady downstairs who has required an ambulance at least three times since Mike died, but who has returned to her husband every time, too, a little slower, but still walking on earth, a serious temptation to the sin of envy for me. As in, *Hey, lady, why aren't you dead and why isn't my husband still alive?* Better than memories around every corner and that stack of papers on his desk, the substance of things you do after your husband dies, after he goes: the bills for sending his body to Florida to be buried near where his parents and sisters live, the bill for his casket, for the grave, for the headstone on which your own name is also etched.

It's all still there, of course. But for a while—just a little while—I won't be.

First stop after Birmingham is Charlotte, so here we are, racing to the gate, then a couple of hours later we're in JFK in New York, surprised by how dingy and cramped the airport is. We don't stop for much except Burger King, we just keep going because we have yet another plane to catch.

Do not give to a child to make him drowsy.

Nice try, Benadryl.

We sleep over the Atlantic, some more soundly than others. My daughter, across the row, has a new best friend, an older Spanish woman named Lupe, who is returning to Spain after a visit to her grandchildren in Texas. For most of the way she chats in Spanish to my daughter, which is good practice for Katie, who is in her fourth year of the language in high school. She even adds a new word to her vocabulary, although its meaning is a mystery. She tells me as we disembark: "It was something like, 'balle, balle'—she said at the end of sentences. I don't know what it means. I've never heard it before."

Yet learning always comes with a price and the downside is that Lupe is pretty wound up about the grandkids so she hardly ever stops talking, not when my daughter has earphones in watching a movie, not when she closes her eyes and leans her head back.

Katie tries to make the best of it, tries not to mind.

"She was nice," she said. "She let me lean my head against her shoulder for a while when I was sleeping."

Well, at least someone slept, even if it didn't happen to be me.

When we land in Barcelona, the returning Spaniards on the flight clap briefly—a sharp, pointed sprinkle of sound through the cabin that reminds me of flamenco dancers.

The Barcelona airport is sleek, clean, and wide open, an embarrassing contrast to JFK, and nearly empty not long after dawn. The slimy egg and cheese biscuit offered on the plane had satisfied no one, and so in a small food court, we found the first of what would be countless pastries for breakfast over the next two weeks. At this point, pastries for breakfast are an amazing treat.

At this point.

It's two, three hours maybe until our Alitalia flight to Milan. We settle to wait on a row of seats next to a wall of glass through which we can see palm trees and in the distance, the mountains that surround the city. An enormous billboard for a clothing chain stretches above the full length of the window far above us. The model's flowery dress and blond hair flow artfully in the breeze. A man is stretched out on the seats on the far end of our row, below her. He's shaggy and bearded, covered by a dingy blanket, his belongings—not in a suitcase, but crowded under some plastic—are strapped to a cart next to him. He looks settled. He even looks at home.

~

These European travelers like to shrink-wrap their luggage. The service—to prevent theft, I assume—is planted in the middle of the ticketing area before security. The suitcase spins and great sheets of plastic whoosh around and encase it. It's a satisfying sound, that *whoosh*.

In line, Michael is asked a question in Spanish by someone in a group in front of us. I don't know what the question is, perhaps what his name is or where he's going. He answers with the only Spanish he knows:

"Uno, dos, tres . . ."

The Italian at the Alitalia counter rubs Michael's head—the Italians everywhere will do this a lot. They tease him and tell him he must get up on the luggage conveyer belt. He tries to oblige, raising up a leg before he's stopped. Everyone laughs. He looks at them, puzzled. He was only doing what he was told, after all.

On the plane, the man across from me makes the sign of the cross as we leave the ground.

By Milan—the last stop before Palermo—we are staggering. There has not been one complaint, not a single tantrum or argument, and I'm proud of them for that, but we are fading, and although no one asks *Why are we doing this? Could we just have stayed at home?* I couldn't imagine that they weren't thinking it. I was.

I go off down the corridor to the shops so I can find the gadget that my laptop needs for Internet access in Italy, and I return to find the three of them sprawled across seats, asleep. I stay awake and dully study the very tall woman, made taller by her stiletto heels, standing impatiently near us, holding a small white dog. She's not tired. I am. She's very well put together. I'm not. I wonder why she's going to Sicily. I wonder why I am, too. Not regretfully, but curiously. *Why am I doing this, again?*

Oh, that's right. Mike died. That's why.

The boys and Katie are awake enough to walk on the plane, then promptly all fall asleep again. So I'm the only one awake in the air, the only one to follow the Italian coastline south. The only one to see Sardinia and Corsica, fully, shaped below, and I feel like I'm studying a great map. The only one to see the water flecked with white. The only one to watch us fly lower and lower, enormous stony crags jutting up, looming ahead.

We're there. We're here. We're in Sicily.

~

But again, why?

I really have no idea anymore, but somehow, Sicily happened. Italy has obsessed me since my first trip there—to Rome—all of three years previously, but I knew nothing about Sicily itself, and barely (I admit) knew where it was, since those large islands in the Mediterranean tend to meld in my head—Sardinia, Corsica, Sicily, Malta . . . Crete? Which was which?

The more I studied up on it, though—taking breaks from late-night marathons of word games on Facebook, games that I couldn't stop playing for that first month but haven't even wanted to touch since—the more intriguing Sicily sounded. I had thought briefly about going to Tuscany or Umbria. Pulling a Frances Mayes. Such a cliché. No one I knew had ever been to Sicily, though. I would be unique. There would be castles and puppets, the websites said. There would be gelato—for breakfast, the guidebooks said!—there would be beaches and great ruined temples where the kids could pretend to be gods and heroes, and there would be a big, huge volcano: Mount Etna.

So yes, we could have traveled anywhere in those empty summer months, but the United States struck me as an unending swath of enemy territory. It was bad enough driving around Birmingham: *We looked at a house in this neighborhood the weekend before he died . . . he liked coming here on Friday nights after work . . . there's his office . . . this is his route, taking Joseph to school . . . behind those trees, around that corner . . . the YMCA.*

There was that, but even out of town, even in other states, I couldn't see anything not being about him, even if we were somewhere he'd never been. There would be sports stadiums, and, because we always took in a ball game when we traveled, there always would have been that sad silence as we passed one. There also would be characters we'd encounter and he would delight in imitating (if he were here), there would be Mass, there would be monasteries or shrines. There would be family or friends waiting to see us, wanting to see us, and at every stop we would be asked how we were. I would answer them, I would say words, but I would never really know what to say. If we stayed in our own country, the place where we all had lived together, it would just hurt too badly because wherever we'd go, he wouldn't be there. We'd see things, but mostly we'd see that he was gone.

The engines slow and whine, and even the sleepers sense change. They stir, rub their eyes, and look out the windows.

I'm a traveler among a crowd of them on this plane, just like I was on the four others I've ridden on the past day. Lots and lots of travelers. We're here but not all of us are. Some of us are gone.

In all of our ways, I'm sure now that what we're doing is looking. All we're doing is trying to understand why someone who was there yesterday disappeared, faded, hasn't returned, or never showed up in the first place. We're all in the plane together, traveling somewhere—anywhere—trying to find where they went. We do all kinds of crazy things on the way: we get lost; we look in corners, some well lit, others dark; we try not to laugh; we laugh too much.

The Palermo airport appears below me—just a couple of airstrips, it looks like, right along the sea, overshadowed by big hulking rocks that could either be monsters or protectors—take your pick. You have to land just right, I also see. You could smash into one or tumble into the other if you're not careful. Or you might land right in between those rocks, still upright, ready to keep going. Safe. This time, and at least for now, safe.

2

T HE PALERMO AIRPORT IS SMALLER THAN THE ONE WE left back in Birmingham hours and hours . . . and hours ago, but it's practically identical. We could be here, we could be anywhere.

The boys lean on me as we wait for the oval track of the luggage carousel to grind to life. They're always leaning against me, it seems, pushing their hard little heads and sharp little elbows into my side, my hips, my legs. Sometimes, I must admit, I want to push back, but I don't. To push back, to push them away? That would probably be bad.

Katie's found a bench where she can sit and yawn. I envy that bench right now. I'm not in pain or collapsing, just very, very tired. All I want to do is lay my body down, stretch it out flat. I cope with this yearning to simply skip the present for the sake of a better place in the future in the way I do: I remind myself that this, too, shall pass: *In two hours we'll be where we're supposed to be and I can lie down on a bed . . . two hours ago we were in Milan. Not so bad. It goes so quickly. See?*

The ritual holds me steady right now, but when I run the gauntlet between past, present, and future at other times—which I do frequently these days—I'm not so much grounded in hope as sunk in mystery.

Five months ago, he was alive. A year ago, we were just moving to Alabama. He turned fifty last November. It seemed so old to us and we laughed about it. But now, it just seems criminally young. Our little boys are just four and eight; they could have known him for decades, but they won't. Or will they? Do they now? God is here with us now, with Mike now too, and in God there's no time, so does that mean that it's all really over? Or is there even such a thing as "over"—at all?

So, yes, sometimes it helps to think about time, not trapped in a little brown bottle carried by me, but carrying me instead. But other times, it doesn't help at all.

~

We're not alone here in the airport, of course, and my curiosity—never latent for long and perhaps better more accurately called "nosiness"—comes to life as I muse about what brought these people to this particular spot at this moment. It's another mental tic of mine: scanning a crowd at a ball game or concert, contemplating people in line at the bank, and imagining what could have brought each of us here.

There's a street corner near our apartment building where a red light forced me to stop on my race to the hospital that day, the longest drive of my life, longer than if I'd hopped in the car and driven to California. As I waited for the light to change, the dreadful, impossible possibility of Mike being dead struck me particularly hard—right in the stomach—and sitting there, it was a new kind of agony, something I'd never expected, and never known before. Now, every time I stop at the light—which I do almost every day—I glance at the cars beside and ahead of me and I wonder. *Why are you at this corner? Who are you going to see? Are they alive or dead? What news did you just hear?*

Specifically here at the Palermo airport, still at this early stage of the trip in which I was still carrying the prejudices of online conventional wisdom that disparaged Sicily as a travel destination, I wonder again. Sicily, I had kept reading online, for all its delights of history, food, and the sea, was apparently an island made of garbage, decorated mostly with graffiti and, in a phrase that stuck with me, suffered an "infrastructure inhospitable to tourism." So with all of that in mind, just who are you people? Why are you here, willingly subjecting yourself to the squalor apparently awaiting beyond these ordinary airport walls, in this place that is so not-Sorrento and not-Tuscany?

This was before I learned the simple, obvious truth that Italians—especially northern Italians—head to Sicily in the same way midwesterners go to Pensacola or Orlando. Sicily is a very popular holiday destination for other Europeans too, Brits and Germans especially. Lots and lots (and lots) of Germans. In fact, I'd be taken for German more than once in the days ahead.

The bags from our Milan flight start their tumble down the track. The boys stare at an old man who has stepped away from his chattering companions and is now peeling off his shirt so he can pull a new one, fresh from the package, over his bare chest. The tall woman from the Milan airport who mocked me with her poise totters about on her high heels, her tiny scampering white dog on a leash. She wanders, glancing occasionally at the circling carousel. As she nears the door leading out from baggage claim, we're all jolted by thunderous barking from two large cages along the wall. She hurries in the opposite direction and the little dog, now in her arms, keeps up the good fight, yapping valiantly at the drug dogs in the shaking, shrouded cages.

~

Bags retrieved, drug dogs skirted, it's now time to get a car. For that is how we will get ourselves around Sicily—in a car. The conventional wisdom again tried to scare me off by pointing to the mythology about Italian drivers, and even an acquaintance who lived in Rome was doubtful. "Really? Are you sure you want to do that?" he asked.

But how else could we do it? Sicily is a big place, we'd be in every corner of the triangle, much of it rural, and I didn't want to be hostage to bus and train schedules and routes. So I'd drive us around Sicily, sure. How bad could it really be?

I doubted the truths of the stereotypes, but I was still nervous since it became clear to me as soon as I started the search for a rental car in the spring that a manual transmission would be an inevitable part of my Sicilian future. Of course automatics are available, but they're much more expensive to rent in Europe, and an extra twenty euros a day would add up over the course of two weeks. I usually manage to stay firmly planted in a frugal travel mode from planning to about two-thirds of the way through a trip, at which point I just start thrusting whatever currency I can dig up at people so they will transport us or supply us *right now. Please. Prego. Pronto. Whatever. Grazie.* Cue whining children, cue Brink of Chaos.

So there in April, at my computer in the apartment at Birmingham, the manual seemed doable and even advisable. I had, indeed, driven a stick shift ages ago, but I couldn't reconstruct the process of actually doing it in my head. You push what pedal when? I also had vague memories of being scared of rolling backward on hills. Sicily has hills. Maybe I should practice.

I didn't know anyone with a stick shift in Birmingham and was actually at the point of going to a car dealer, claiming the desire for a test drive, when I got my chance a few weeks before our trip, but not in Alabama. By late May, the Indiana house had finally sold, so we drove up there to give it a final cleanout of what we'd left the previous summer—a basement full of things, plus some furniture that wouldn't fit in the apartment.

For a couple of days, I would sort and clean, call in the St. Vincent de Paul thrift shop truck for donations, meet an acquaintance who worked for the diocese up there who had agreed to take many of the books off my hands, and finally, to meet movers who would haul the rest down to Birmingham. The boys would play in the yard and in the empty rooms, Katie would stay with the friends she'd not seen in almost a year. It would be fine. Nothing to it. Loose ends.

Except for the fact that so many of those loose ends were Mike's. His yearbooks, his photos, his files of his old writings, most of his CDs, and souvenirs from his fifty years of life filled those boxes in the basement. His sports caps: Marlins. Gators. Jaguars. Bucs. His Florida teams. He hadn't needed that stuff right away, after all. There wasn't room for it in the apartment. He'd come back for it, that was the plan.

So I sorted and wept, unpacked, repacked and cried some more, drying my eyes and forcing enthusiasm when the boys would race by with some discovery from the yard or a toy from a closet's forgotten corner.

While still in Indiana I tended to the driving-in-Sicily issue. A neighbor had an Audi that she offered for a trial run. I took a break from the boxes on the last morning we were there, puttered around the block, and discovered that it came right back to me, with only a jolt or two before the drive smoothed out. I thought I had forgotten, but I hadn't after all.

A few hours later that day, we drove (in our own car) away from the house, now emptied of the evidence that any of us had ever been there except for maybe faint crayon marks on a kitchen wall. We were all crying, and it is hard to say why. It wasn't as if we were leaving him behind. He wasn't back there, after all, and what pieces of him that were there, we were taking along with us. We didn't even mention him by name.

If he had been with us, it would have been pure celebration in the car—his car, the better car—the burden of the unsold house lifted, another chapter closed—a good chapter, but now a better, warmer one with only one housing payment instead of two beginning. It would still be warmer, expenses would still be halved, but he wasn't there. We wanted to move on, but we wanted to move on with him. I wanted to remember it all, but I wanted to remember it with him.

Turning that corner?

Now *that* was hard driving.

~

"I can give you automatic."

We have gathered our bags, found the car rental office across the parking lot—helpfully marked with RENT CAR in ten-foot letters painted on the building—the boys and Katie are exploring the restrooms, and I'm listening to the young man behind the counter, who is speaking that universal language called "upselling." He's fluent. I understand him perfectly.

He even anticipates my objection to upgrading to an automatic.

"Only eight euros more a day," he offers, tapping the paper he's laid out between us.

Smooth.

Thirty minutes in Sicily, well-behaved children lined up on a bench behind me comparing restroom notes—pretty exciting stuff—a beautiful day, and already the frugal traveler is tempted.

"Very good," he says in his thick accent after I give in. "And is Mercedes, not . . . *Punto*." He practically spits the name of the cheap little Fiat brand. There's no "practically" about it, actually. I think he does spit it, just a little bit.

~

Katie holds the map and navigates from the passenger seat in the front, clearly a little worried about the strange road, the different numbering and signage systems. I'm not. If it's not a maze of an American subdivision of identical houses where I'm searching for a birthday party or sleepover site in dusky half-darkness, I can usually figure things out. We're headed to Scopello, which is north on the coast, and we are driving north on the coast, so we will eventually hit it, even if our map fails us. It's only about three in the afternoon. We have time. No big plans. Nothing but time.

And now, just five minutes in, easily managing all kinds of bends in the road, I feel something.

Happy? No. I am not sure what *happy* means these days. But *pleased* might cover it right now. The Mediterranean is a brilliant blue on our right, the great, porous-looking craggy hills are on our left, the rippled surfaces looking as if the rocks had been dripped from the heavens by the children of giants playing on their massive private beach called Sicily.

I'm just glad we're here. That I'm here. I'm driving, moving, heading somewhere new. This place is different from anything I've ever seen and it reminds me of nothing at all. I like the contrasts outside my window between gray stony rises and deep blue smooth seas, and after all my questions and doubts, I feel the possibility of enjoyment. I want to see what happens next. It might, it strikes me, be good.

And as this interest in the future, in what lies around this curve on the road arises, so does, just as quickly, an immediate, habitual mental correction. You might as well call it survivor's guilt. I do.

I don't really know how I'm supposed to act, what I'm supposed to think about life since he died. Am I allowed to laugh? What does it mean if I do? What does it mean if I edge up on joy while doing something in a place I wouldn't be if he were still alive? If the only reason I'm in Sicily is because he's dead, and being in Sicily turns into a good thing, does that mean it's good that he's dead?

Even before Mike died, I wondered about such things—about chance, about the good that wouldn't have happened unless tragedy had struck someone, somewhere. A former student of mine was a young wife and mother of a four-month-old a decade ago when her husband was killed in a car accident. Since then she's remarried, borne another child, and her online postings tell of a busy, happy life. They also tell—once a year—of tears, still shed, all these years later. I always think I should ask her how she works it all out in her head, but I never do.

Mike was buried in St. Augustine, Florida. We stayed in a hotel in the old city, and during some downtime, my daughter bought, from a vintage store, a dress that she would wear to the prom later in the spring. It was tea-length and turquoise, with an Asian flair. It suited her beautifully. A couple of months later, I took her photo in it before she went off to the dance and I thought, *She would look different today if Mike hadn't died.*

This stupid life, in which grace, loss, sadness, and joy are intertwined and even dependent on one another, in which the living are here because others were born and eventually buried, in which we look different because someone died, in which beauty is born of suffering, mystifies me. I can't sort it out. I just don't know how I'm supposed to feel.

Death has no more power over you.

St. Paul preached that all the time. What does that mean? That we will rise again? Yes, but I think it's also about how we keep living under the shadow of death: specific deaths, our own death, and death in general have all kinds of power over how we live.

Death where is thy victory? Death where is thy sting?

Paul could mock death. Me, I'm not there yet.

———

I don't think Joseph is pondering any of this as we wind our way up the coast, but then maybe he is. It is hard to tell with him. But for right now he seems interested in the now. He's studying the landscape outside the car window, and without the prodding of any painfully cheerful educational leading questions from me, he comments on how blue the Mediterranean is, and how the light hits the rocky craggy hills and how they look gray, then pink, then green, and how the shadows of the clouds dance across them.

He turns to me.

"When can we go to the beach?" he asks. Adventure beckons. He seems to be ready to follow it, to listen for it, to find it. His excitement seems far less complicated than mine. But then, just like his grief, it always has.

~

Mike died on a Tuesday. We buried him in Florida the following Monday morning and were back home in Birmingham that same night. Everyone went to school the next day, because honestly, what else was there to do? I wish I could have gone to school, frankly.

A few days later, on schedule, unconcerned with death, Friday did its thing and showed up.

Almost every Friday, around five or so, on schedule, Mike would stride into the house, ready to party with our boys.

"It's Fun Friday!" he would announce; the boys would shriek, and we would go out to eat—unless it was Lent—or to some kind of sporting event if one was happening. Maybe both.

That Friday, that second Friday without Mike, I picked the boys up from school. Katie had play rehearsal and wouldn't be home until late. I had no intention of doing Fun Friday, because the concept seemed not only absurd, but even disrespectful.

But as they climbed out of the car that day, the decision happened, and I didn't make it. Joseph had connected some dots in his head. "Hey, it's Friday! Can we have Fun Friday?"

Fun Friday? What? Really?

We stood at the bottom of the stairs, they expectantly, me stunned. "Do you *want* to have Fun Friday?" I asked, carefully. Mostly for my own sake, carefully.

"YES!" they shouted, and ran up the stairs, ecstatic.

I followed them slowly, confused. A half hour later we were at the wings place near our apartment, at their request, on that first Fun Friday without Mike. As they always did, they asked for quarters and raced to the video games. I sat there, alone, an unopened menu in hand in the same half-light, the same table, the same waitstaff, the same greasy air and din and televisions that had surrounded us every other time, every time in the past, every time with Mike. Here and then, now and . . . *where?* Time settled in layers around me, thick layers, full of shadows. *Two Fridays ago we were here . . . next Tuesday it will be two weeks . . .*

So I cried. The poor little waitress. Just like the poor hairdresser a month or so later. And the bank teller a bit after that.

The boys played on as they waited for their burgers. Sometimes, I admit, in those early weeks, I looked at them when they were grinning and laughing and I thought, *What is wrong with you . . . your daddy died. How can you live like this, here, now? Don't you get it? Stop it . . . be sad.*

I never said any such thing, of course. I just watched and tried to learn, because you know what the Man said:

You must be as a child.

Must? Really? *Must?*

~

One evening a couple of months later, four-year-old Michael sat in his father's chair back in our room, pushing off on the desk with his little foot, turning the chair and himself in it around and around. He had a prayer, he said. He'd made it up himself, he said. What's the prayer, I asked?

"God," he crowed, "we will see you in NO TIME, then we will be with you ALL THE TIME!"

And he pushed off again, spinning.

3

OUR PARADE INTO THE CENTER OF THE VILLAGE COMES to a halt in front of a beige stucco three-story building with a wood-frame door and a hand-painted sign. *Pensione.*

Just like it was in the pictures. Except—not.

I though I knew exactly what this pensione looked like. I had studied photos and memorized the glowing reviews, after all. But as much as it was clearly the same place, it wasn't. The photos had revealed a general shape of things—a three-story building, a green-colored door, a bottom story with a sofa and fireplace and desk where a woman was now conferring with a couple on the right and a scattering of dining tables on the left. Yes, I had seen that picture, but it had not brought me closer than that ink on paper or pixels on a screen—couldn't bring me into the embrace of a real space, thick with wood and photographs and murmured voices from the kitchen in the back or the clean, spacious bedroom up a flight of slick marble stairs.

The place existed. For weeks it had existed in the form of an image. Now that I was in it, the image was gone and I never thought of those pictures again, only the real experience of it, solid and warm, with something new to offer every time I walked in.

My back and shoulders ache to be relieved of what the suitcases and bags bear. In one of those bags—the purse slung over my shoulder—is stuffed a large wallet. Slipped in between other important documents in that wallet is a photo of Mike. Him in a blue-checked shirt, a Jaguars cap, close up, grinning into the camera.

I wonder about reality overtaking the images. Does the reverse happen, too? What happens, what is left to love and be surprised by, when reality shifts and fades and all you have left is a picture slipped in between the passports, the papers that have allowed you to travel so far from home?

~

Elena owns the pensione and she surprises me, too. She confounds the entries in my Mental Encyclopedia of Sicilian Stereotypes by being neither short, stumpy, and swathed in black nor tall, lithe, and wrapped in Versace. In fact, she's not Italian (by birth) at all—she's Chinese. She'd grown up in Panama, where she had met her husband, who was originally from Scopello and grew up in this building, his family home. She shows us a photo on the wall how it looked fifty years ago: an abandoned-looking hovel standing in the ruins of southern Italian poverty.

But now here we are, in the middle of new photographs of a more prosperous time, a place transformed by travelers of all sorts: travelers who left home and met other travelers and returned and built something new out of the old, travelers who have come here to see what the other travelers have done. Coming, going, meeting, making new lives out of what seems like chance.

~

We collapse into our beds, made up with crisp white sheets and nubby white coverlets. Katie and Joseph have the bunks, and Michael and I are in the double bed in the same airy room that's open to the outside by a large window with only shutters and no glass. Through it, as everyone is settling down and before I lie down with Michael, I look down to the cobblestones, across the way to the two streets full of small buildings there, and then up a hill to some half-constructed holiday villas, abandoned for the moment. There aren't many people about in the late afternoon. I don't know who's here besides us—here in the hotel, here in the whole village. I have no idea. I can't see the Mediterranean, but I know it's there, around the other side. I lie down to rest, thinking that I would try not to sleep, that I would try to stay awake.

No chance. I'm startled from the depths, not by noise, but by smells. It's garlic, it's tomatoes, it's something frying. I know that if I'm smelling food, it must be around the announced dinnertime, which is eight. I despair for a minute—thinking at first that perhaps we've even missed dinner, and, second, that there is absolutely no way I am going to get everyone back to sleep tonight after this rather monumental three-hour nap so late in the day.

They are roused, they rub their eyes and find their shoes, and as we descend, I remind the boys about manners. Remind? Not really. Threaten? Yes. We tread carefully on those slippery steps, and I whisper my litany on the way, pausing for Katie to study the collection of books arranged on shelves at the turn of the stairs. *Be polite*, I say. *There'll be pasta, there'll be gelato later, but right now, there might be fish. No matter what, be polite, even if it's an octopus on your plate. No faces, no complaining. If you do, no gelato tonight . . .*

We continue down to find our table, marked with a card with our room number. Katie lays down the book she's found for her later enjoyment: *The Plague*.

As it turns out, I didn't need to worry about the little boys and their food. Elena had asked in an e-mail about the boys' relationship to fish, and since I had to admit that it's not a good relationship, she was ready and waiting with chicken cutlets for this first night. They paused before digging in, though, to watch wide-eyed as I got my lesson in skinning and deboning a whole fish. Elena stands at my side, reaches in, and delicately strips John Dory—festooned with capers, tomatoes, and a sprinkling of parsley, lying helpless on a solid white plate—of all that held him together in one piece, since I myself have no clue.

The boys' culinary boundaries are indeed tested, though, and tested even before John Dory makes his appearance. The *primi* is penne, and the sauce is a familiar tomato, but what I don't mention is what Elena had told me earlier—that there would be swordfish and eggplant as well. You can taste it—even smell it—just a bit. There are chunks of swordfish here and there. Eggplant. I look around my table, table number 4.

Well, here's the thing: somehow, traveling for about twenty-eight hours straight, having only picked at airline pasta and a slimy airline breakfast biscuit after chicken nuggets at the Burger King in JFK, gives a kid an appetite, makes him so hungry that he'll scarf down a whole plate of pasta, eggplant, and swordfish included. He's hungry. Whatever you put in front of him—it's gone.

~

Hunger came to mind a few weeks before. I was reading what St. Francis de Sales—a seventeenth-century bishop and spiritual writer, the patron saint of writers, as a matter of fact—had to say about widowhood in his *Introduction to the Devout Life*, and I was resenting it. He said that a devout widow should accept her lot and not even think about finding another husband. Such a thing is not at all on my mind—I can't imagine it, don't want anyone in my life in that way if it can't be Mike—but I still chafed at his words. Why not? I wondered. Don't oppress me!

For in those first few weeks and even months after Mike died, I hungered. I starved for his presence. I looked for him constantly and for a time, I even tried to *be* him. I suspect that's what I was doing, anyway.

Just a few days after he died, I decided it would be a good idea for me to take his job in the diocese even just for a year or so, if the bishop agreed. Mike had a good vision for the Office of the New Evangelization, I understood it, I believed in it, and I could make it happen. I could also use the health insurance.

That grand plan lasted about a week. Maybe less.

For those few days, I sat—mostly idly, dreaming—in one of

his offices in the chancery downtown, across from the cathedral. Mike had scored two offices for himself as befitting a man who had somehow absorbed four or five jobs: one across the hall from the bishop's, and the second on a lower floor, less accessible, where he could actually get some work done. So I sat in one or the other of those rooms, surrounded by notes in his handwriting, using his calendar, pushing around his hairbrush in the top drawer, trying out his energy bars from the bottom drawer, looking up to see the photos of us on the bookshelves, his brown sport coat swinging on its hook on the back of the door every time someone would come in or leave.

One day during that time, I went out to lunch with the bishop and some others from the office. It was at the Magic City Grille across the street from the chancery, the steam table heavy with fried chicken, creamed corn, greens, and biscuits.

It was very pleasant, lunch, but as I sat there, I sank, and I sank hard. I didn't want to do this, at all, I discovered. I didn't want to be here. I wanted Mike to be here and then come home and tell me about it. And the conviction dawned, at first slowly, but then with more force: *Do you really think Mike wants you to do this? Would he try to do your job if you died?*

And then, frankly: *Do you think that in a million years, Mike would wish this on you?*

Probably not. Actually, not at all—he wouldn't wish it on me at all. He'd lean forward, look me in the eye, and say, "Are you *nuts*?"

So there it was. He had died, and that was it. What a fool I was to pretend to keep him alive, especially by sitting in his desk chair, flipping the pages on his calendar, taking his calls. It was also wrong, for he wasn't God. None of us are. His life on earth was over, his mission—whatever it might have been—accomplished.

I wasn't comforted when I tried to absorb his life. I wasn't fulfilled. I was hungrier than ever.

When the other set of eyes that helped you make sense of

the world, when the one who held the mirror that helped you see yourself so much more clearly, when your best friend and companion is here one day and just gone the next, you can feel like you're starving. So perhaps St. Francis de Sales had a point. Maybe you should hold back, he was saying. Now is not the time to eat too fast. Sit with the hunger for a while. Give it to God. What is it I'm really hungry for anyway?

At dinner that first night in Scopello, I turn a corner in this small world and find a couple from Atlanta, here with the husband's British parents. Atlanta—two hours from Birmingham—and here we all sit, skinning a fish in Sicily.

There's also a Danish couple, with whom Elena converses in German, and finally, an Italian couple with a five-year-old named Michael. And they call him "Michael," pronouncing it as we do in English. I attempt to ask the wife at one point what the Italian for Michael is and she tells me—*Michele*—and I say, "But you call him 'Michael'"—intending it to be a leading question, since I don't know enough Italian to more than lead, but she just nods cheerfully and doesn't explain why, mostly because I wouldn't understand anyway.

They are from a town outside Venice. After dinner, we sit in plastic chairs outside on the square. Katie has gone up to the room to read *The Plague* and sleep after remarking with pleasure and surprise, "This isn't at all like *Fawlty Towers*!" The boys are wide awake because they have found their new friend—several, in fact, for not only is there the Venetian Michael, there are other village children, and there are dogs. The boys race madly about in the piazza, around and around, up on rocks and down, to the fountain and back, chasing each other, chasing the dogs, being chased, roaring and squealing like the Grand Prix is speeding right through Scopello.

In that darkness, we talk as well as we can—the husband

speaks a little English, the wife none. This is a good vacation, he declares—away from the television and the video games, where his son can just play outdoors, create and imagine, where they can escape from all that noise and routine.

I didn't bring us to Sicily to escape. Well, not really. Okay. But even if it were total, absolute escape I was after, I have already clearly failed. Southerners are here, parents concerned about their children are here, Catholics are here, and of course, I am here with my memories, layers of time and space pressing on me, me pushing back.

It's hard to believe that we have come all this way in so short a time. Where were we this morning—Barcelona? Spain? The nap refreshed me, dinner was wonderful, the wine has relaxed me.

And I'm feeling . . . full. Perhaps even near bursting, not with great joy, exactly, but more with awareness and interest, curious about life here in this tiny village of forty-five regular residents, of what we might see here and beyond tomorrow. I'm interested in these Venetians, these Danes, these Sicilians by way of China and Panama.

I'm here, seeing all this, ready to explore and learn for many reasons. Some I know—Mike died—and some I don't. All the reasons—especially the main one—*Mike died*—continue to confuse me and fill with me doubt and that constant undertow of survivor's guilt.

The sky above is clear, even with the light behind me, softly glowing from the open windows and doors of the pensione; I can study the sky above as I listen to boys shouting, dogs barking, and the villagers and visitors walking, laughing, murmuring in the square.

Bodies glitter in the heavens. Some I can see, and others I can't.

I can't see them.

I just can't see him.

What hits me is hard, but familiar. It's right in the gut and it's all about the empty space, beside me and inside. It gnaws like a hunger, it leaves me gasping like a thirst.

But then further beyond that empty space, a few steps beyond under those same glittering heavenly bodies, visible and invisible, little boys run and stumble on cobblestones, leap off ancient stones, and, when they are thirsty, run to the fountain in the piazza that trickles and flows day and night, that never stops. I watch them as they run to that fountain, drink deep of that water without hesitating, and then quenched, satiated, satisfied—race back into their game, laughing.

4

LEAFING THROUGH THE *ROUGH GUIDE,* THE *BLUE GUIDE,* and *Fodor's* on this Wednesday morning, I'm thinking, but not terribly hard. Thinking about today, about tomorrow. Everyone else is asleep—Katie and Joseph quite soundly on their bunks, Michael less so. They slumber on through the steadily brightening light, through the voices and cobblestone clattering coming through the open window. Apparently every single one of the forty-five permanent residents of Scopello conducts their morning business outdoors, in the street, under our window.

The basic plan for this first, full day after the Insanely Long Journey had always featured not much more than resting and situating. It seems like an even better idea right now because Michael is feeling puny, as we say in the South. I touch his forehead again. He's still a little warm. I'm still leafing and pondering, the morning lopes on, and he eventually rouses that slightly warm, sluggish self, slips off the bed, and heads to the bathroom, this time without the urgency of his previous visits this morning. Those first three sessions must have cleaned him out.

I rouse myself to get my phone, check the time (still in the Alabama zone), do the math, and come up with ten o'clock. I take the two steps over cool tile floor to the bunks and nudge. Joseph stretches. I speak and shake a bit, and Katie responds. She doesn't move, but she does mutter, which is something.

I don't know the rules of any B and B including this one, so while I hope breakfast is still available, whether it actually will be is a mystery. Well, we'll eat whatever is down there, however it's offered. Then, if Michael's up to it, we'll venture out, see the village, and maybe find the sea. We'll see the grander sights of northwestern Sicily that the books assure us can't be missed tomorrow. Today we'll just live here in Scopello, I think.

Seconds pass. A couple of minutes.

Michael.

Where is he? Still in the bathroom? I call. No response, no movement, not a peep or rustle or clank. It's silent in there. I push open the door. He's stretched out on the floor, curved around at the base of the toilet, unmoving even when I call his name.

Michael?

He still doesn't answer. His eyes are closed, he's perfectly still. *What was I thinking? To bring them here? Why?*

~

Grief means sadness. Everyone knows that. But what you might not know until you live it—I didn't—is about regret, and how in the world of grief, sadness may be the air you breathe, but regrets are the cracks in the ground that trip you up and knock you flat.

The regrets hit me immediately, and hard, the day Mike died.

After that cryptic phone call, I was seated in a little room where they wouldn't just tell me what was going on for the longest time, but where I also knew that he was dead because there was absolutely no urgency in how anyone was dealing with me. There was no hurry, nowhere to go, no one who needed me there now.

Finally, they told me, and the nurse took me to see him.

It was a large space, tiled all over, floor to ceiling. The cabinets were shut tight now, machines pushed aside, the floor shone, freshly cleaned. I listened for echoes of earlier chaos, wondered what fluids had spilled on the floor.

He was lying about twenty feet away from the door. My last hope—that this was all a mistake and this "Michael" whom they wanted me to see would not be him after all, that he was at the office all this time—shattered.

Lightly covered by a blue sheet, he looked as if he were sleeping.

For five minutes, maybe ten, I stood there. I leaned, pushed, against the door frame, moved forward a bit, slid down and sat against a tiled wall, let the nurse put her arms around me. I received a plastic bag with his wedding ring and crucifix necklace in it. I snapped my cell phone open and shut, open and shut. I thought; I was besieged by thoughts and images and notions; I battled. I said his name over and over; his name filled my soul.

I studied him from that door frame and I thought I saw his chest move. I would have sworn to it, that maybe I even saw him swallow. I wanted, more than anything else, to talk to him about this. I wanted to tell him that I was looking at him and they were telling me he was dead, and I wanted to hear his smart remarks in retort. I wanted to ask him, if he was, indeed, dead, what he was thinking right now, and what he was seeing, and if it was really all true.

I wanted to ask him what I should do now.

The nurse tried to pull me toward his body, but I resisted. From here, it was safe to believe that his chest was still moving.

I opened and shut my phone, over and over. I thought about telling people about this, about Mike being dead. I wondered if I should take a picture. I wanted to, and I almost did, but then I didn't. I wondered if they could still harvest sperm, or if it was too late. I wondered what I would do with it if I got it, and how fantastic and sad it would be to give birth to another child of Mike's in a year or so. Even in those few minutes, I could see her. I could see that it would be a girl.

So I stood there, stunned, and I stood and didn't take a step toward him. I couldn't move away from the wall. Thinking back, I don't know why I didn't go right up to him, look at him, touch him. Maybe it was because I was essentially alone and afraid. If a friend had been with me, they would have taken me up, would have stood next to him with me. I could have gone, in that case. I would have, willingly.

But there against the cool tile, under the indifferent light, it was just me and the nurse who was doing her best but who was, through no fault of her own, not a friend, but an enemy, for she had led me into this terrible place. Because of her, I found my husband lying there, dead. I couldn't trust her.

Whatever the reason, whatever held me back, I regret it now; I regretted it the minute I got into my car that day. I drove out of the parking deck, was immediately immersed in midafternoon stop-and-go traffic, and considered turning around and going back, to see him again. But I didn't. I just kept driving to Joseph, who was doing whatever second graders do on Tuesday afternoon at Our Lady of Sorrows School. The day before yesterday, we'd sat in the balcony there in the church next door to the school, the huge pietà in bas-relief looming over the altar right in front of us: Mary cradling her dead son in her arms.

But me? I didn't do what she did. I could have moved closer and even embraced Mike, but I didn't. Nothing rational was holding me back. It was only fear.

For he was right there, you know. For years, he was there, close enough to touch. He was an opinionated and strong personality, but a good listener and wise and he loved me. But I always held back, just a little. A private person, an only child, never quite sure of total acceptance, even from him, so I held back.

And now, I am so, so sorry; and now I am helpless to do anything about it, about any of it, about how close I got to him that day and the many days before that when I was happy with him but the edge of my cynical melancholy always lived in the shadows, casting doubt. What had I missed because of that? Well, too bad. I'll never know. It's over, it's done, it's just too freaking late.

I can work through the sadness. It's right there around me,

on a crucifix—his—hanging around my neck, in the Sorrow-
ful Mysteries of the rosary rolling around, getting tangled up in
my purse, in the stained-glass windows of Our Lady of Sorrows.
They depict Mary's sorrows—*dolours*—which are not a sentimen-
tal recollection, but a reference to a specific devotion: seven sorrows she experienced during her life, beginning with Simeon's
prophecy. Simeon, who told God he could go in peace now that
he had seen the Messiah—yes, that Simeon—also told Mary that
her heart would be pierced. Her first sorrow.

So when I go to Mass, I stare ahead at Mary embracing her
dead son, and I'm surrounded by those windows depicting all of
her sorrows; and the one that looms most vividly—at my left as
I sit, no matter where I sit—depicts the corpse of Jesus under a
sheet lain out flat on a slab. It's enormous, it seems to be double
life-sized. When I walk by, I'm close enough to reach up and
touch him.

So yes, the sorrow I get. But who's the patron saint of tears
of regret and missed opportunities, unspoken thoughts and un-
breached walls?

⌒

Michael! Michael!
He finally answers to his name, opens his eyes, and leans his
head against me as I sit on the clean tile floor and hold him so
close to me, rocking.

"I was just tired," he murmurs. "I wanted to take a rest."

⌒

The four us make it downstairs by eleven and there's our table,
with the room number on a card, just as it was last night at dinner, except now the dining room is empty. Our table is the only
one still laden with waiting food hours after everyone else has
come and gone

The food looks lovely, and I feel terrible, but perhaps the staff is used to it, as travelers sleep off the road and the air and get adjusted to a new place. There's bread, marmalade, oil, butter, cheese, muffins, yogurt, blood orange juice strained into ruby-red clarity. Perfect round plums from their own tree.

The boys ask for milk from the woman—not Elena—who comes out from the kitchen, and we all absorb the cultural diversity lesson of the day as huge cups of warm milk—*latte*—are presented to them; I learn right then and there to specify: *latte freddo. Si. Freddo. Cold milk. Grazie.*

After breakfast—brunch?—Michael perks up and declares he is ready to take a walk. But we are barely out the door when he makes a different declaration that leads right back to the bathroom, but nothing really happens there. We head back to the room just in case, but around one, our hostess Elena calls up and delicately inquires as to how long we will be in our room because, you know, the ladies need to clean.

Well, he can lie down in the car as well as on the bed, I say to myself and then to everyone else. Katie and Joseph agree. They're more than rested and ready to get out and about. I stuff bathing suits into the backpack and extra clothes—and a couple of plastic bags. We walk through the village square in the bright early afternoon sun. Michael certainly had a rocky start this morning, and walking beside me over the cobblestones, holding my hand, he's subdued. But he might feel much better in just a little while, and I want to be ready for that. I want to enjoy the day, I want to be prepared to enter into it, to not miss a thing.

Today, I don't want to have any regrets.

5

W E'VE LEFT THE VILLAGE AND ARE HEADING A LITTLE west and a little north. Various possibilities lie ahead. Zipping around curves, rising over gentle hills, I contemplate options. The nature preserve just north of Scopello? A little farther on, the Greek ruins at Selinute or the beach town of San Vito Lo Capo?

The road takes us through a number of small villages that all seem to pop up out of nowhere. These concentrations of one- and two-story buildings, all connected, crowded close up to the road, bright purple and pink flowers cascading from balconies over beige and pastel walls, offer no warning that they're about to appear. Back home, gas stations, convenience stores, and ice cream shops always signal that more civilization lies ahead. Mike liked those ice cream stands, especially, and he always insisted on stopping at one, and always when we were just about an hour from home. It drove me crazy, to give in to his insistence that we stop and sit at a picnic table to eat ice cream when we could be putting more of the trip behind us. I never wanted to stop.

I would stop here, though, and poke around a village or two, but in this late afternoon, there's no reason to. In every town, the sidewalks and streets are empty, shutters, gates, and doors are shut up tight, as Sicily rests for the *reposa*. The silent towns appear in front of me and then just as quickly recede. To each other, we're just a blur.

Near the beginning of the drive, I'd taken one wrong turn. I'd thought that the road up the coast leading to the Zingaro Nature

Preserve would pass right through and continue up the other side, but it didn't. It stopped right there, and since Michael clearly wasn't up for a nature walk, this road had become, instead of a destination, a dead end to be left behind.

So many roads. So many places to go. So many ways to get to wherever it is we end up. Where we will end up this afternoon depends on such odd things: one boy's stomach, the other boy's need to run about, the interests of the girl with the map, a camera, and *The Plague*. The weather. The traffic. What's open and closed. And of course, the driver's whims. For that is about all I've got to offer today: no plans, only instincts and vague desires.

What will we remember tonight as we settle down to sleep? Will we be grateful or will we lie there, restless, second-guessing ourselves, wondering what we could have done differently if we'd just waited and taken the next turn instead?

⁓

If only. There's another regret for you. I thought about that a lot for months and months. What could I have done differently? What could have made a difference? What road was out there that might not have stopped, so abruptly, at such a dead end?

Mike's death certificate told me that the cause of his death was "cardiac asystole." I had no idea what that meant, so of course, when in doubt, go online. In the course of my research, I encountered a striking phrase in the title of a medical journal article. I thought the three simple words were the fruit of an Oliver Sacks–like medico waxing poetic, but as I encountered the phrase in other places, other papers, other articles, I found that wasn't the case. It's a real medical term for the ultimate dead end, for death itself:

A dismal outcome.

A few weeks after Mike died, after doing all that fruitless research that told me nothing helpful (because all "cardiac asystole" means is that his heart stopped; it says nothing about *why* it stopped), I was waiting to get the oil changed in what had been his car. I riffled through papers in the glove box, finding not much of interest, just maps, receipts, and ticket stubs to races and football games. What I'd expect to find.

And then something else: a printout of a web page, folded into quarters, dated at the bottom from the previous winter, a year ago, when we were still living in Indiana. It was information about some sort of cardiac test, and the doctor had scribbled a note on the bottom to Mike, suggesting that he go for this test.

He never did, of course. I know that for certain.

What would have happened if he had? Various people who know about such things have told me that it's very possible to have a complete cardiac workup in which everything looks fine one day, then have a heart attack the next. *You just never know* is what people always say.

The autopsy didn't tell me anything either because, well, there wasn't one. My extensive medical education, gained through hours of watching *ER* and *St. Elsewhere*, had led me to believe that autopsies are standard issue upon a death. I found out after weeks of thinking that surely an autopsy result was going to be coming to me soon that it was not. The attending physician told me that if Mike had been found collapsed in the locker room, yes, there would have been an autopsy, but since this was a "witnessed event"—in the middle of the workout room at the YMCA—there wasn't, unless I had requested it.

But then, nobody asked me if I wanted one either.

So I'll never really know. Not that it matters in the end, really. Does it?

Well, it could be worse, too. That thought—*If Only*'s evil cousin—gives me a perverse kind of solace, knowing what regrets I *don't* have. I don't have to regret that he didn't receive good care, for he did. His heart stopped working—for whatever reason it did—in the middle of a busy workout room in a YMCA, with a defibrillator close at hand wielded by people trained to use it. An ambulance was there in minutes, and he was taken to a fine university hospital. It's like the doctor told me, "We did everything we could do. If it was going to happen anywhere, that was the best place, short of the hospital itself."

So no, he didn't collapse in all the other places he could have: in the slightly off-the-beaten-path workout room at our apartment complex or while he was running around the little lake across the road, hidden from sight, both places where he might not have been found for a while. If that had happened, my regrets, my *if onlys* would have been even more profound and absolutely unanswerable: *What if someone had found him?* I would think over and over, every night. *He would still be here.*

So yes, I wish he'd had that test, I wish I'd known to ask for an autopsy, and I'm glad I don't have to imagine him alone, needing to have his life saved with it actually savable but with no one around to help. But the regret and wishes for alternate histories and the chance to go down another road can only go so far. It was his heart. It failed. Knowing exactly what valve or artery failed doesn't change a thing. *It is what it is*, he used to say about other irritating matters, about life itself. It is what it is.

A dismal outcome.

~

After about thirty minutes in the car, Michael seems to revive a bit. He asks for water, he wants to know when we're going to get there (wherever we're going), and he and Joseph started poking each other in the backseat. Yes, all better now. Running around ruins might push him a little much, but sitting in a fresh sea breeze? That might do, and not just for the supposedly sick one, either. So yes, we'll go to San Vito Lo Capo, which sits on a little horn of land that juts out, pointing to Sardinia. Katie holds up the map and shows me the way.

A couple of kilometers before we actually arrive, we encounter, up a hill and around a bend, a fairly large square stone structure topped with a cupola, standing in an otherwise empty stretch of gravel above the sea. It looks old. It even looks religious. So of course, I have to see.

I pull up onto the gravel beside what turns out to be the shrine of San Vito himself. The boys want to stay in the car, so Katie and I get out and read the sign printed in both Italian and English that tells us the story of San Vito.

He was, the legend says, a young boy who came here after escaping from Diocletian's persecution of Christians in the early fourth century. Upon landing, he immediately started preaching the Gospel to the natives. The legend continues, in a twist that reminds me of everyone from Jonah to Lot's wife, the inhabitants of the area refused to listen and were, as a reward, buried in an avalanche. Vito was accompanied by his nursemaid, Crescenzia, who for her part could not resist looking back at the devastation and was turned to stone on this very spot.

But, it is also said, this same Crescenzia had the power to drive away devils, a power that can be accessed here at the shrine. You do this by grabbing some pebbles from the ground and tossing them into the arched opening, through the metal grate, right into the tiny dark space within.

So Katie and I do this. We look around, take pictures, and scoop up pebbles from the ground, driving away the demon spirits.

Go away, devils.

Go away.

Who can resist throwing rocks? Joseph can't, and he appears at my side, ready for his turn. Michael's calling me from the car, so I leave Katie and Joseph and go to him, and he informs me that he think he might throw up. I whisk him out of the still-clean car and he squats in the dirt, coughing and spitting, hacking and whining, but not outright vomiting. A few yards away at the shrine, Joseph is still interested in the ritual at hand, but hesitant. Throwing rocks into historical structures, especially those that have something to do with God, is not something he's normally encouraged to do. Katie and I both start giving him instructions. She says, and I shout a little, because I'm farther away, still tending to Michael. "Throw a pebble in," we say. "Toss in some rocks!"

Michael's sniffles turn into frustrated wails. Crouched there on the ground beside me, he looks up, pink cheeked, his huge eyes watering. He pleads, if not for his life, for his sanity in the midst of his crazy family.

"I don't wanna!" he cries piteously, almost begging. "I don't wanna put rocks in my mouth!"

Oh, the poor child, what could he be thinking?

What is WRONG with this woman? She puts me on planes for twenty-four hours, eats a whole fish in front of me, and now she wants me to eat ROCKS?

~

My husband had a wooden shadow box—not very big, smaller than a shoebox—full of relics: tiny bits of cloth snipped from the garments of saints or touched to things that had touched them all glued on lace-edged oval cards and pinned to the backing in the shadow box. He had holy cards with faces and prayers of and to saints. And he had a couple of flasks of holy water, all this arranged on the top shelf of a bookshelf in our room.

Along with the holy water, he had oil. It was, specifically, St. Joseph's oil from the huge, enormous hilltop shrine to St. Joseph in Montreal. The shrine was inspired by the healing and prayer ministry of Brother André Bessette, now canonized a saint. Brother André would slather the sick and the suffering with this oil, and the abandoned crutches at the shrine testify to healing. Mike scored his flask of St. Joseph's oil when we went to Montreal on our honeymoon after getting married in a church called St. Joseph's down in Florida.

In those first few weeks after Mike died, yet another *if only,* another regret took hold of me in the form of an admittedly peculiar fantasy. I relived that day in my head—it's what you do, you relive it constantly, retracing your steps, *ifonlyifonlyifonly* pounding like another heartbeat. I imagined myself getting the call from the hospital. If I'd been thinking—really thinking, I scolded myself—I would have grabbed that St. Joseph's oil. I would have walked into that room, bravely, not cowering. I would have strode right up to him lying under the blue sheet, I would have taken the oil, rubbed it on his forehead, on his chest, and who knows—oh, who knows what St. Joseph, what God might have done? Who knows? He might even still be here.

So yes, I would imagine this, and I would regret it one more time, because it just seemed to be one more part of the unending regrets about lost chances, dead ends, and dismal outcomes that perhaps didn't have to be so dismal.

But then I would look up at that crucifix, and I would listen to the prayers I was saying, and I would think about love, about the empty tomb—because it was Lent and Easter was coming—and what I claimed to believe about all of it.

And I would be forced to wonder how a scenario featuring me rescuing him from being perfectly known, loved, and accepted by God forever fit into all that. The point of the relics, the prayers, the point of my life being that the dismal outcome is not so dismal after all.

But Jesus healed . . . I would argue.

But then we shall see face-to-face . . . I (well, St. Paul, actually) argued back.

Those regrets. They are . . . bedeviling.

Can somebody hand me a rock?

~

Half an hour later, the Boy Whose Mother Tried to Make Him Eat Rocks has recuperated nicely. He and the others are doing what you'd expect at a beach, transitioning into the Kids Whose

Mother Hauled Them Across the World at Great Expense Just So They Could Play in the Sand.

We'd parked right across the street from the beach. I could find no hint of how to pay for the spot, so we just left the car there, hoping for the best. I haggled for two large towels from a sidewalk vendor and was pleased with myself for bringing him down by ten euros, but then was immediately and predictably afflicted by guilt, thinking that the African immigrant was probably more in need of those extra ten euros than I.

As we settle in to our spot on the chairs we rented for five euros—discounted because it was the end of the day—an American introduces himself after overhearing us wonder where we might change our clothes. He's an expat living in Prague, vacationing here with his Czech wife, and he directs us to a restaurant across the way. The owner—who'd lived in Philadelphia for a while, as it turns out—allowed beachgoers to use his restrooms to change.

And now I'm watching the boys from my five-euro chair, watching them dig up sand, pile it up, and cheer as it washes away. Some days they're crushed when the sea takes their creation, but today destruction delights them. Katie drifts between us, sometimes lying in her own chair and reading, sometimes going down for a swim, sometimes joining the boys, digging up the seashore. The boys race back up here to me once in a while, mostly to remind me of what I'd gotten wrong in my pretrip learned pronouncements about beaches in Sicily:

"You said the water would be really warm because we're close to Africa, Mom."

"You said we'd probably have to wear water shoes because the beach would be rocky, Mom."

Well, you know what? It does a child good to experience his parents' ignorance once in a while. It does.

It's crowded here, but not people-to-people packed. I hear all sorts of accents, including other Americans—more than I'll hear at any beach in Sicily, as a matter of fact. Just like any beach, teen-agers wander in packs, the girls giggling and glancing at the boys, the boys pushing each other in the water and throwing things.

The vendors at the edge of the beach selling towels were only the beginning of the San Vito Lo Capo sales force, I discover. For this beach is crawling with people—almost all Asian or African—selling things. Guys stumble through the sand under the weight of long rods strung with plastic toys across their shoulders. Other guys pick their way around sunbathers, carrying racks of jewelry, piles of purses and bags. A small Asian woman, struggling with a folded table, offers massages. A fellow selling "Indian Tattoos"—henna—totes his table and his huge notebook of designs through the rows of sunbathers.

Coconuts, too. Cut in half, in wedges, coconuts are the only food or drink sold on the beach. *Coconutcoconutcoconut . . . cocococococococo . . . nut . . . Uni Euro Coco . . .*

So all that's different. What's also different is what I see people eating here on this beach: nothing. No one has hauled big coolers of food and drink along as you see on American beaches and it occurs to me that I certainly hope they wouldn't, consider-ing the expanse of Italian meals. I once joined a group in Rome for lunch; it lasted three hours, and I got the impression that this was just another normal day. God knows, these people don't need to snack.

They do smoke, though, in numbers you wouldn't see on American beaches, so I suppose the bad habits even out some-how. I once asked my son who lived in Rome for a time why it is I never saw a Roman woman under sixty who was overweight. "Because," he explained, "they all walk everywhere and they all smoke."

Speaking of women, I'm struck by the lack of one-piece bath-ing suits. Every single woman of every age is wearing a bikini. For the men, the rule is obviously: the older the fellow, the skimpier the suit. Teenage boys and young men run in their baggy trunks, but the older men, bronze, weathered, glistening, walk and talk in that stately way with their hands clasped behind their backs, wearing hardly anything at all.

It's hot and sunny, but the breeze is just right. There's an enormous outcropping of rock looming over us, just behind the beach that will, I'm thinking, look great in the pictures. I take some.

It's a complete day, apparently redeemed from the difficulties of the morning by the sun and the constancy of the sea.

Some things are the same here, some are different. What's mostly different is that Mike isn't here to play this game with me, to compare this place to the other beaches he loved (because he loved beaches too), to tell stories about South Florida, to pick out the strange characters, imitate them, bring them into his repertoire, to file his son's determination not to eat rocks into the family history.

I think of all that, and along with it, I ache for him, but because I'm imagining what he would do if he were here, I also hear him saying what he would say about the ache, about a dismal outcome, about regrets about what I think I could have done.

What you meant for ill, God turned to good.

It's what Joseph—one of the other Josephs—says to his brothers of their betrayal. It was one of Mike's favorite, defining scripture passages. His motto, you could say. Working in the craziness of the world, of the church, it came in handy. Understanding life, it was essential. Oh yes, he would say it now. He would say it a lot.

But still. Who wouldn't rush for the oil? Who wouldn't throw rocks at the demons? Who wouldn't, being told that if you got on the treadmill at that moment, you would die in ten minutes, step off? Who wouldn't regret and wish that life—given by God, after all—had not ended?

But then there's Jesus on the crucifix, dead himself.

As usual, I don't know what to think or feel. I want Mike back, and I feel guilty and faithless for that desire. I run over the alternatives in my mind—what could have happened—but then I try to confront what love is. What it really is. In pieces, I can see it all, but I'm absolutely unable to pull it all together. Just when I think I have, I see something: an elderly couple, walking hand in hand down the beach; Katie wading into the waves, carrying Michael on her hip and holding Joseph's hand.

And then it all falls apart, once again, punctuated by questions and regrets and cold absence. Funny how absence looms and emptiness blocks your view.

But I'll try. I'll try to push it aside, try to work through it again, because I want to see.

I want to see the four-year-old down near the waves, the little boy who began his day curled up on cold tiles made of earth and stone.

Now he's digging energetically through grains of sand, those tiny specks that were once pebbles and before that, rocks—perhaps even great ones like those looming behind him right now. His hair ruffles in the breeze, his eyes are bright and focused now, glinting in the late afternoon sun. He gathers up handfuls of ancient sand, shapes it to his liking, and out of those million tiny stones, he starts to build something new.

6

THE MEDITERRANEAN IS BACK IN VIEW THIS THURSDAY morning, but too far away to touch at the moment. We're standing atop a mountain on Sicily's west coast, a low wall the only barrier between the four of us and a rough tumble into the vineyards and olive groves directly below.

That wall and my grip on Michael's wrist, that is.

Beyond the vineyards and fields, the city of Trapani spreads between the base of the mountain and the Mediterranean. We study the sea; I point out the shadowy Egadi Islands a couple of kilometers offshore beyond the city; and finally we squint and shade our eyes, look south, and try to spy Africa. It seems that from up here standing at Erice's town wall on top of this mountain, you should be able to because it seems as if you can see the world. If you needed to, you would be able to spot attackers long before they arrive over the waters; you would have time to ready the defenses and since you are so close to the heavens, you could call on the divine for help and protection. *Il velo di Venere*— the veil of Venus is what they call the cloak of clouds that often shrouds this mountain, especially in winter

Up here, you can see what's coming at you. You have no excuse not to prepare.

❧

I have left the little white car in yet another ambiguous parking situation. It's down there somewhere in a near-empty lot that seemed to be related to the gondola station at the base of the mountain.

The large, friendly fellow who emerged from a group of men gathered under a canopy at the edge of the lot as I pulled into a spot after successfully navigating through Trapani, my first Sicilian city, seemed legitimate, although I really wasn't absolutely certain at the time and I'm not even sure I would bet on it now. He grinned at me and held out his cupped hand.

"Quanto?" I asked—one of the Italian phrases I'd made sure to know, along with *dove* (where?).

He answered with a shrug. This wasn't in any phrase book, but it was universal and I got it: *whatever.*

The (almost) fresh-off-the-plane tourist was still packing nothing but the twenties and fifties from the airport ATM, none of which this guy was going to get. I held up a single euro coin.

"Okay?"

He nodded, still friendly. I had apparently not insulted him, which just might be good news for the car.

But as we swung up the mountain in a scrappy yellow capsule hung on a cable, flying past the ghosts of the Carthaginians and Crusaders who preceded us to the summit, I started to worry. I remembered reading about lot squatters—basically fake parking lot attendants—common in Sicily. And why would he take a little more than a dollar for a parking spot at a tourist destination if he *wasn't* going to steal my car? And what if there was, indeed, a legitimate parking lot authority around there that I was supposed to pay but hadn't?

We stumbled out of the gondola car at the summit and started walking along the walls of the triangle-shaped town of Erice, stopping here where we can look down at the vineyards and fields, the city and, somewhere down there, the white speck of a Mercedes, maybe sitting in a parking lot, maybe speeding along city streets in the hands of a happy new owner. The possibility that my car wouldn't be where I'd left it dogged me all the way up and all the way down—and it would worry me a lot here in Sicily over the next two weeks, since I never—not until the very last full day—grasped the parking procedures. Would the car be there when we returned? Would we be stranded in Trapani? Would I have sold them my Mercedes for a single euro? Well, lucky them. At least it is not *Punto*.

~

Walking along the southern wall of Erice, four-year-old firmly in hand, Katie and Joseph ahead, I'm struck not only by the views down the mountain on my right, but also by the solidity of the grays on my left. Sicilian buildings up to this point—two whole days!—have settled in my memory as a variety of pastels, but Erice is very gray. Gray stone buildings crowding against gray cobblestone streets and alleys, gray steps leading up and down and in between. Its medieval nature—most of it was built in the fourteenth through the seventeenth centuries—is preserved and undisturbed and it's spotless. No trash and, of course, no graffiti—the scourge of Italian walls, generally. It also seems untouched by people living and working in the twenty-first century. It's just too quiet.

But we're here for castles, not to conduct business, and Erice has a couple of those. One, the Castello di Venere lies straight ahead at the end of this side of the triangle, its battlement towers looming at the edge of the mountain, a fortress clinging on the tip of a fortress. The little boys are ecstatic, and they race up the graceful loop of wide stone steps leading to the gate, shouting of knights and dungeons.

Predictably, that gate is closed. No hours are posted, no indication of when it might be open again.

Not that I hadn't tried to warn them. The guidebook had said that Castello di Venere has varied and arbitrary hours, and—I'd explained before we came, having experienced it in Rome myself—in Italy, you really can't count on anything being open when you hope or even when it's supposed to be. (Sorry, Italy, but you know it's true.)

They're disappointed, but not crushed, and their spirits definitely lift not long after we turn away from the town wall and head back into the center when, without even trying, we stroll right into the kind of place we always like to be, no matter what continent: a park.

The green space under trees, traced with walkways and dotted with playground equipment, is the Villa Balio, built by a count in the nineteenth century, and it is spread out front of the faux castle he also built. (No admission into this one, ever, according to my book.)

A fellow with a cart and a miserable-looking donkey stands on the small plaza between the count's castle and his gardens. The animal slouches in the increasingly warm sun, weighted down with traditional (or is it stereotypical? What's the difference?) flowery regalia, as is the cart, as is the man, who plays accordion and sings songs you think you should hear in Italy. Or the Olive Garden, at least.

I manage one photo before he notices me and starts motioning with his mouth and his hands in a pantomime of eating. *I have to eat!* he tells me that way. True enough, and I respect that. I do. Ah, but this fellow wants five euros—he holds up his hand, five fingers spread, to show me—for a lousy photograph and I'm not feeling that today. I only paid one for a few hours of parking (I think), after all. Five euros for a picture? No, *grazie.* I make a show of putting away my camera. He shrugs—*whatever*—and sings some more, shifting his gaze to the small group approaching from perhaps their own thwarted attempt to scale the Castello di Venere.

The boys are over the castle, though, and are excited enough about the perfect little park in the trees on the mountain as they home in on the obvious first choice: a small round red metal ride that operates on the same principle as Disney teacups: you sit facing the middle, grab the disk in the center, and twist and spin. So they do this. And as they spin, they are Luke Skywalker and Hans Solo, they are pirates, they are—I shouldn't even have to mention it—knights. All these toys, these rides scattered through the small park on top of the mountain—the spinner, the slide, the swings—are bold blues, reds, and yellows, primary, basic and strong.

Katie wanders off, the hungry man with the cart and the donkey sings over by the villa, and I consider that I have come all this way so they can spin around, swing, and slide in a park on top of a mountain, both of which—mountains and parks, even a park *on* a mountain—are available back home, in Birmingham, Alabama.

As per usual, I feel guilty about the trip and the expense, guilty and privileged, no more than a faux Christian, not bearing a cross, but leaving it behind, storing it in a closet along with other relics, hopping a plane and running away just because I can afford to.

But still, I'd rather be here than there. Right now at least, I'd rather be here, in this park where the no-plan within the plan within the shocking jolt has brought me. Spinning, swinging, sliding, climbing, the world spread out below us, heaven so near. Here is fine.

~

While the boys spin, Katie swings, another mountain—Monte San Giuliano—looms as a backdrop across the valley. I watch her and can't help but wonder what she's thinking about. It's only a few weeks before she begins her last year of high school. Knowing her, a highly intelligent young woman of mostly optimistic temperament and a strong will, I'm guessing that she's thinking good things about what's ahead for her. She has her plans, even as they change; she has her varied dreams—of theater, of politics, of indeterminate good times stretching indeterminately into the future—and like the upward arc of her swing, they will surely just happen. It will all work out.

It's what all of us think. It's what I thought. It's probably what the guy with the donkey thought, too.

Something close to a weird, slight panic seizes me as I watch her on the swing. Have I prepared her for coming back down? Have I told her enough times—*You never know what will happen; you'll be disappointed, even crushed; you'll end up in places where you never planned to go and you'll wonder how you got there. Be ready.*

Oh, our plans. What folly, for really all we are is lost. By ourselves, we can't see a thing for what it is.

Have I told her this? Have I made sure she gets it? That she knows to ask for help, to listen to God above any other voice—to really *listen*?

That life—all life, including hers—is a riot of plans and regrets, of being found and lost, and, God willing (and he is), found again, that nothing will go as planned, but—in the final ironic mystery—if they had gone in the way I had planned for myself, if I had not suffered the terrible, sad regretful things that I did when I was in her stage of life—that she would not be here, swinging?

~

After hanging out in the park for half an hour, we start looking for food. We wander the maze of narrow medieval streets, free of cars but thick with souvenir shops. Unlike the castles, they are open, and unlike most of the churches up here (we have found), they don't charge you to come in and look around. Just like any tourist site anywhere in the world, each bursts with shelves and racks of goods identical to those of the shop next door, all variations on the local theme. Here it's Pinocchio pencils, puppets and dolls, it's the *trinacria*—Sicily's three-legged symbol—on every object you can imagine from plates to key chains. It's flags and maps of Sicily; it's Sicilian ceramics, swirling with yellow and blue.

Erice is pleasant and pretty, the meal we grabbed at a cafeteria of sorts, pizza and *arancini*—rice croquettes stuffed with ham—was very good, and the pastries at the famed Pasticceria di Maria Grammatico were even better, especially gobbled up seated at a tiny table—the only table on a small rear balcony of the shop, cream dripping from cannoli and pastry nubs and dots glistening with dark fig filling.

So yes, I like Erice well enough and I'd love to be back to see it at night or during cooler weather when the mists and fog descend, as well as dig through the churches and museums we won't be able to see today, but right now, as pleasant as it is, my dissatisfaction returns and I feel as if we're actually strolling in a rather large open air museum under this warming sun, which of course, is not the worst thing in the world.

It's not Epcot, but it's also not Rome, with its living layers where you study fallen columns a block away from banks and design firms, as Vespas roar on the road behind you. As I look around in this spotless relic, I compose wry, knowing blog posts in my head about this, about the interesting questions Erice raises for me, about living museums, about the importance of accepting that times change and about living in the now.

In front of a rack on a gray stone wall displaying buttons and magnets, Katie stops and points, amused, to a row of magnets featuring the smiling face of President Obama, right next to some pretty-delicious-looking resin cannelloni.

I chuckle, then like a reflex, my mind shifts and I'm thinking without trying or even forming these exact words, *Oh, that's funny. If Mike were here, he'd laugh and we would . . .*

I know. *I know.*

~

We wander a bit more in this late afternoon, poke our nose into a few more shops, buy a couple of Pinocchio pencils. I don't want to go crazy on the souvenirs just yet. We don't want to weigh ourselves (meaning: me) down this early in the trip. We also finally find some open churches that evidently aren't important enough to charge admission. They're all made of stone, quiet and old, a little ramshackle with wooden benches and crucifixes and candles.

And in each one, Padre Pio finds us.

I knew he was popular in Italy—this mystic stigmatic Capuchin saint from southern Italy, friend of the poor, the sick, who bled with the wounds of Christ, who could see souls as they were, behind the façade—but I was still surprised to see him in every single church on this trip, almost every day, beginning here in Erice, where he blesses us from pedestals, plaques on walls, and stickers on car windows.

In one tiny, empty stone church in the middle of the gray stone town, we find small vigil lights in red plastic stacked in a box next to a side altar. I finally have more change from paying for lunch, so we toss some euros in a small dish. The clatter of the coins echoes against the walls. We take our turns lighting candles. The boys reach up—I hoist Michael in my arms—and they place the candles alongside others, already burning, scattered on a stone side altar in front of a photograph of Padre Pio, and as we always do when doing this thing—light candles in a church—we pray for Daddy, because that's what he told us to do, and more than once.

"When I die," he would tell me at odd moments, "don't ever stop praying for me." He said that a lot. He despised funeral canonizations that presumed the deceased was already in heaven, especially since one of the traditional purposes of a Catholic requiem, or funeral Mass, was to, you know, pray for the dead person's soul, which everyone knew needed it. He understood people, he understood himself, and he knew hardly any of us die a saint. Even saints don't die as saints. Mike died running on a treadmill and several people remarked that they could imagine him closing his eyes and then opening them, finding himself running straight into God's embrace, and I could too, but still.

Before my friend Molly died that same year, I visited her in

Florida. She knew she was dying, and she was struggling with all kinds of feelings about that, but she also said outright that she wanted to go to purgatory. She leaned forward as she told me this, almost like she was poising herself to run there.

"I *want* to go to purgatory," she said fiercely. "I want everything but love to be burned away. Nothing but love left in me."

Don't stop praying for me.

So in the gray stone chapel, our coins glinting in the shallow white bowl, tea candles flickering in red plastic cups, we pray. There with Padre Pio, who saw a lot of things we can't, we pray to God, who sees even more, who sees every bit of it, who sees us as we are and waits for us from the mountain where, they say, and I try to believe, everything but love has been burned away and a feast awaits.

❧

Just a few minutes later, after leaving that little church, turning this way and that in the maze of streets, the day starts to crack. One moment we're free-spirited wandering tourists—a bit melancholic, true, but still brightened by the sun and the adventure—and then the next moment, Michael has been tripped up by cobblestones, he's crying hard that his ankle hurts and he can't walk, and looking around us, I am pretty sure we are lost.

Lost—I didn't think it was possible, for each side of the triangle that is Erice is no more than a kilometer long, but the twisting and turning, even with maps, got me flipped around. I thought we were headed for the gondola station, but we weren't—or maybe we were and just a few more steps, around one more corner, would have taken us there, but either way, right now we feel lost, Michael is crying, it's hot, we're all tired of walking, and just like that it all turns. We don't want to be here anymore. We want to be somewhere else. Just like that.

❧

What is it like to be seven years old, home from school, playing with Legos, vaguely wondering where your father is and when he will get home, wondering why your big brother has showed up from Atlanta in the middle of the week, and then be taken into your mother's bedroom to hear that your world has not just cracked in places, but collapsed?

I can't imagine. And I was there. I gave Joseph the news, and I felt my own pain, but I can't imagine what it feels like to be him, to have your world shatter in that particular way that it would for a seven-year-old.

Of all the bad things about the day Mike died, telling Michael and Joseph was the worst part, especially to Joseph because he was older and he understood. It was one of the worst moments of my life, to have to deliver such very bad news to such little boys.

So why not couch it in good news? In *the* Good News?

I could have done that. I could have said, *I have to tell you that Daddy's heart stopped today, but it's really okay because he's with God in heaven now. We're happy about that, so let's praise God, okay?*

I didn't say that. Oh, I may have said it in a way, but I didn't tell Joseph to be happy. Since I was crying, what sense would that have made? I didn't tell him to be happy because it would have been nothing more than a slap in the face. Another one.

I also know that as Catholics, we give sorrow its due. The Good News doesn't blow off the bad news. It transforms it. But in this life, practically speaking, on this earth, at least, we still hang crucifixes and we still come to a pietà, head buried in our hands; we still sit in Our Lady of Sorrows, the corpse of Christ lain out on a slab at our side.

To brush off the absence, to show the son the cool, heavy, shrunken body of his father in the casket and tell him simply to be of good cheer? Some people might do that. I didn't.

Death is conquered, yes. I believe it.

But even Jesus wept.

7

S O WHERE IS IT? WHERE IS THE DAMN SALT? IT'S SUP-
posed to be around here somewhere—big heaps of it on the
flat plains leading to the sea—but the salt obviously hates
me because it's hiding.

The way I figured it, after finding the gondola station up in
Erice, swinging back down the mountain, and best of all, finding
the car waiting for us—even after all that, it was only a little past
three, so we still had time to see the salt. Yes, that is exactly the
way I figured it before I started driving in circles. Now? I'm not
so sure.

And why am I determined to find it, to see the salt, to show
my imprisoned children hills of Sicilian salt? Who knows. Perhaps for the same reasons that we'd try to see cotton fields in Mis-
sissippi, lobster traps in Maine, or a Ford plant in Dearborn. Salt
harvesting was historically a vital part of the Sicilian economy—
it's less than minor now, as is the case with another former pillar,
tuna fishing, but I'm thinking that it would still be helpful in understanding, you know—Sicily—to see it. We could certainly live
without beholding it in situ and possibly be content with studying
a jar of boutique Sicilian salt in a souvenir shop, but really, we're
so close, it will only take a few minutes to find it. Why not?

The glitch is that I am just not finding it right now. I know
it's there. I know that Nubia is the name of the salty town, and
it's just a bit south of Trapani. It should have taken ten minutes
to reach it. But I'd left my large, beautiful detailed map of Sicily

back in Scopello, and it takes more time than you think to drive in circles many, many times.

I eventually do find that salt though. After U-turns and three-point turns, a return to the autostrada—twice—I finally land on that elusive road closest to the coast that I knew was there all along, that I remembered from my map. I find Nubia, drive through it, see a sign for the "Salt Museum," and finally—big piles! Of salt! How tall do you think those mounds are? They must be fifteen feet tall! And look at the tiles layered on top of the salt! Can anyone tell me what those might be for?

"Look at the big piles of salt!" I cry.

Katie makes learned, vaguely interested noises and the boys stare out the window.

Clearly, it's time for the Salt Museum.

It's in an ancient stone building with a windmill. An also ancient, finely dressed woman in a suit and heels inside takes a few euros for admission after assuring me that yes, there are English-language placards inside.

We drift around the two large, high-ceilinged rooms that are filled with beams, levers, gears, and nets once used to gather and dry the salt. I must presume this is so, since every description but one is written in Italian. I think that if I were to concentrate on the placards and the equipment and the diagrams, I could probably sort out how everything was used, but that would require more energy—far more energy—than I have right now. Because you know what? At this point, I just really don't care.

So after ten minutes, we're done with the Salt Museum, the boys and Katie have been photographed in front of the salt mountains and we begin the drive back.

What did they learn? I'm not sure, except that big piles of salt in Sicily are sadly not for climbing and that the way from Trapani to Nubia, Sicily, is surprisingly long and involves, again surprisingly, a great many circles.

❧

Because, you see, I tried very hard during those forty-five minutes of searching to not let on that I was lost. Even Katie, deep in her book, was only a little bit aware of my frustration, which probably struck her as not really distinct from my normal, everyday level of frustration with life in general. So why did I pretend? The same reason I always do: they've got enough to worry about. Why should my uncertainty and confusion become theirs? Why should I disturb their momentary peace with my problems?

❧

But of course, I was, indeed, lost. Just like at home, back in the apartment, wondering what the hell has happened and how I could ever find a way out of this tight, painful knot of a place, I was lost. Knowing that there was a map somewhere, and a way out, but not able to reach it. And at home, just like I do here behind the wheel, I do my best to hide it from them.

I save most of my tears for darkness and solitude, long after they are asleep or for when they're gone at school. It's then that I can be alone in our bedroom, wondering why I'm alone, trying to feel not so alone, surrounded by his clothes, his books, his music, his photographs, his scent on the shirts still hanging in the closet and even the possibility—on recordings of his mission and retreat talks—of hearing his voice again

So I don't let them see the raging grief, but neither do I lie outright, when the question arises, when emotions run high.

I miss Daddy. They sigh and even sob. *I want Daddy.*

Me too. And together we cry.

To them, right then, I won't deny that I'm lost.

It's complicated, though, too complicated for them to understand. I move about the apartment, drive on errands around Birmingham, drop off from school, pick up, push a cart through the grocery store aisle, all with a purpose, and never wavering from that small purpose, and never getting lost in those particular tasks, but still, when it comes to how to lead the rest of my life, circling.

Once I stepped back from my weeklong experiment in diocesan employment, I found myself puzzling about what to do next. Certainly in the short term, we'll stay here for a while, but then what? We don't have to live here forever. We could move this summer once the lease is up, and we could settle anywhere.

And what about me and my long days? What will I do? I suppose I'll keep writing because I like it, but even before Mike died, I had been feeling a little spent on that score. For fifteen years, I'd been writing on the religion beat—penning columns, then composing blog posts and writing books about saints and prayer and Catholic teaching. After so many pages and so many words, I'd been thinking I was just about done with that, and since February, that feeling only deepened. Without him to be my partner in understanding and processing church craziness and spiritual mystery, I was feeling drier than ever. I really had nothing left to say that others couldn't say just as well, or probably better, especially now since every subject seemed, at its essence, to be about death to me. I felt that all I had to say to anyone, of any age, in any context, was a variation of "Hey, you know what? *Memento mori*, sucker!" over and over, at the end of every chapter. That could get boring.

There's also the possibility of doing something radical and new—like going into missions. People do that. Move to a Haitian orphanage or a barrio somewhere. Or just hit the road. I know a man whose father died when he was young, and his mother responded by selling everything and taking the children on a yearlong trip around the world. Missions? Keep traveling? I play with those possibilities at times, but then I think about the children as they are and in terms of what they need right now—especially Joseph, mourning his father, and I am pretty sure that ripping them away from the school they like, the friends who make them laugh themselves silly and forgetful really wouldn't help. It doesn't take much to see the truth of that. So given my own dryness and my children's needs, what next?

I don't know. Drive the kids to school, sit around, drink a Diet Coke, think about death, go pick up the kids from school, put them to bed, and then think about death some more.

Sound like a good plan?

Well, like I said: lost.

⟿

On our way back east, Erice and the salt behind us, we take a late-afternoon break just before we reach Scopello. The road has taken us up yet another mountain, and there on the ridge is a rest stop of a parking lot, woods, and space to take in the view. We buy gelato and Sprite from the refreshment truck parked in the lot, take our snacks over to the benches against the rail and look down. Dinner is late here and we need snacks. That fantastically bright blue sea lies below us, along with Castello del Mare, the larger town where, Elena had told me, her children went to school and where she shops. Lumps of rocky hills melt behind us, shrouded at the moment by rings of clouds. Joseph is intrigued by the possibility that he, too, might be here wrapped in a cloud, without even knowing it.

There's a large crucifix here at this roadside rest stop. It stands across from the food truck at the edge of some woods. A shelf for candles is tacked to the post below the crucifix. The small sign posted next to it is in Italian, but here I take the time and try to figure out what it says. I want to know why Jesus hangs here, in this spot. I can't just walk away without knowing. It says (in translation):

This humble gift is an offering from Giuseppe Collica to the Christ of the Belvedere so that He might be a light and heavenly guide to Giuseppe's beloved daughter Angela.

The boys jostle with each other over by the railing. Katie leans against it, studying the sea and the town below. I stand in front of the crucifix for a minute more, wondering. So, about Giuseppe's daughter Angela. Was she alive? Had she died? Why did she need Christ's light to guide her?

Was she lost?

～

We leave Scopello tomorrow, so this is our last chance to check out the Tonnara di Scopello, the iconic landmark that comes up near the top when you type "Sicily" in the image search box: a cove protected by a group of large, conical rocks jutting out of the water. I tell the boys that the defensive ships would hide behind the rocks, which immediately leads to excited conversations about pirates as we pick our way down the steps from our car. At some point, a tuna-processing plant was set up in the cove, and while those days are long gone, the building, as well as a small plaza, rows of huge anchors laid out there, and a swimming cove remain in private hands, open as a recreational area and for social events. They filmed a scene of *Ocean's Twelve* here, so Katie and I prepare ourselves for the privilege of walking in the footsteps of Signor Brad Pitt.

There's no beach, but rather a concrete platform where a couple of dozen people—mostly families—lounge and prepare to swim and then later dry off. A brush with bare toes tells me that the water is quite cold here, but the boys decide they'll try it out anyway. They change behind towels, which probably amuses anyone who's watching, since children swimming nude here is not a rare sight. Two men are teaching their sons to swim—one French, one Italian—the little Italian boy is nude but for his water shoes. I wonder, fleetingly, if this will make Joseph sad, to see fathers teaching their sons, but he seems to be too distracted by other discomforts, by chilly water and rocks hurting his feet, to notice or think about it now, that fundamental discomfort in his soul.

～

A couple of hours later, back at the B and B, dinner happens, and it's dreadful. Well, it was probably delicious, but to me it was awful, the only "typically Sicilian dish" that I'd anticipated I might have trouble with myself: *pasta di sardine*. When I thought about what it might be, I envisioned whole sardines scattered through the pasta, and I believed this would be not my favorite, but still manageable with a smile, since I like anchovies, which are sort of like sardines. Right? But no, that's not what *pasta di sardine* is. It's strong stuff: greenish brown, thick with sardines shredded and mashed into a bristly sauce. I get it down—because that's what my mother taught me to do—but tonight I envy the boys and Katie with their plain pasta and chicken cutlet.

Afterward, we get the obligatory gelato in one of the shops off the square, and we return to sit outside the pensione in plastic chairs under the stars. Venetian Michael is there too (in fact, the boys tell me that they'd seen the family at San Vito Lo Capo the previous day), so they play whatever it is little boys play as they run, as they race with dogs, charge to the fountain and back. Whatever the games are that these little boys play, laughing and running, they never get tired. Never, ever tired. And even though they're running in circles, they, for one, seem to know exactly where they're going.

From where I'm sitting with Venetian Michael's parents, I can see the side door of the village church. When we passed it that first day, exhausted and ready to rest, I was interested to see a wheelbarrow outside that door holding this year's partially burned Paschal candle.

A meter or so tall, it would have been lit for the first time during the Easter Vigil, the night that Jesus broke through death. The worshippers would have gathered in this piazza not far from where I'm sitting. There would have been a fire, and the priest would have passed the flame from fire to candle, and he would have led them all into the church through the darkness, past the village fountain, chanting about Christ and light. That light would have pierced the deathly darkness of that night, that deep night of tightly sealed graves, of mothers with empty arms and friends torn by regrets. It would have happened right over there.

I imagine Christ of the Belvedere, a few hills away from where I'm sitting, light and shadows dancing at his feet. Who lit them? Who joined their prayers with Giuseppe's tonight, adding their own yearnings to his pleas for the dying man on the cross to lead Angela to the light?

Now here's what you do with the Paschal candle after Easter: you light it during baptisms, and when someone dies, you bring it out and set it up next to their casket. During the funeral Mass, if anyone can tear their gaze away from the box in the middle of the aisle, they'll see it. They'll see *Alpha* and *Omega*—beginning and end—traced on that tall candle and they'll see the flame dancing in between the body hidden in the wooden box and the other body hanging on the wall. The flame darts around a little, and sometimes, just for a moment, it may even seem to hide, like it's gone out, because that's just what candlelight does. It flickers, it dances, and sometimes it hides.

～

On this last night in Scopello, steps away from where that Easter fire burned, I, with my maybe twenty words of Italian, am talking to Venetian Michael's mother, who speaks no English, so there's a challenge for you. I don't know how it comes up or how we talk about it in a way that we both understand, but for some reason, I get it in my head that I want her to know something about me. I need to communicate this thing that explains me, that explains us, that explains our presence, how we ended up here out of all the places in the world that we could be tonight. I say what I think might be correct: *Mi sposo, morto.*

She gasps, reaches a hand to touch mine, and I work out a way to tell her more about it.

I point to my heart.

8

THE McDONALD'S IN PALERMO EXISTS. OF THIS I AM certain because I just passed it. All four of us saw it coming—Joseph calling it out first since he's always the one to spot the landmarks before anyone else—but not soon enough for me to figure out how to get to it before plunging us even more deeply into Palermo and its legendary traffic.

We're finished with Scopello, have said our good-byes and paid our bills, and are moving east and south, headed to the agri-turismo in the center of the island where we'll be staying for the next week. On the way, we're stopping in Monreale, just outside of Palermo, for a guided tour of the town's *duomo*, or cathedral. The duomo is famed for its mosaics and early medieval multicultural vibe, and I'm interested to see this product of a rare moment in which western Europeans, Arabs, and Byzantines were able to live and work together here in Sicily.

Which is where McDonald's comes in. That's where we are supposed to be right about now, in the parking lot of that McDonald's to meet up with a tour guide named Jacqueline. An article she'd written on a Sicily tourism website about the duomo and specifically why there's an image of St. Thomas à Becket in one of the mosaics had intrigued me—she seemed like a person who would explain the duomo to me in a way that resonated with my interests—so we had arranged a tour, which was going to begin with us finding her at McDonald's. Then what? That, I couldn't say.

Those specifics of how we would all travel from McDonald's

through Palermo and then up the hill to Monreale is still unclear to me as I whip down a Palermo side street, pull a three-point turn, and wait at a light to return to the highway, back in the direction of the golden arches.

Would we abandon our car to the elements and the citizens of Palermo at McDonald's and then she would drive us to Monreale? Would we all hop on a bus? Would she have her own car that we would follow through the city and up to Monreale? Would she take over the wheel of our rental and drive us up there herself?

I didn't know, and she hadn't explained. All I knew is that after a few friendly, informative e-mails, she had instructed: *Meet me at the McDonald's. It's right next to a Holiday Inn.* The juxtaposition of it all—McDonald's, a Holiday Inn, Palermo, us—amused me when I thought about it in the weeks leading up to the trip.

You can't miss it, she'd said.

Well, I didn't, but then I did, mostly because I didn't know how to look. The highway flowed off the coastline right into Palermo. The city, just like those small towns of the past two days, rose immediately around us, the traffic surged, McDonald's popped up on the right too late for me to figure out how to reach it, and I shot right past it.

The traffic courses two or three lanes wide despite there being no actual markings on the road. The cars and trucks flow in and out of interchanges and side roads as the city thickens. It's "gritty." I believe I'm required to say that because, you know, just as Erice is always "haunting," Palermo's "gritty." The traffic? It "teems," naturally. But it's really not that bad, I'm thinking as I try to enter into the Sicilian driving gestalt, which seems to be centered around the ideal of *never stop. Ever.* Except for the purely conceptual reality of "lanes," as well as the toy-hawking vendors who jog up to our windows when we even just slow down, driving in Palermo strikes me as no more fraught with danger than doing so in Chicago or Manhattan, and I've driven in both.

Waving away yet one more fellow with his rack of cheap

puppets, I brace myself for action, for Joseph has alerted me that the multistory Holiday Inn lies ahead. He's right. It's on the other side of the highway, many lanes of steady traffic across from us, and I'm really not yet grasping how I'm supposed to get over there, for I don't see exits or indications that any exist. It's a lot like yesterday, I'm thinking, as I scan the maze of roads for a way over. I can see just where I should be, which is also where I want to be, but the way that will take me there is a total mystery.

~

I was always afraid of death. Petrified. The first time it really hit me, I was twelve years old. Trying to go to sleep one night, death popped up, grabbed me, and threw me down with this truth: that girls who were my age one hundred years ago were now dead and gone and that one hundred years from now, some other girl would lie awake thinking about girls who'd lived a hundred years before them, girls now dead and gone. And one of those dead girls in the nighttime of the living girls a hundred years hence would be me.

Life would go on and interesting things would happen, but that was too bad for me. Vastness of the universe, tiny, insignificant me, the great void of time, and so on.

And so it stayed, more or less, my whole life. The whole *he who believes in me will never die* thing really didn't stick at a deep level. I said I believed it, I wrote about it, I argued for it, and honestly—I did believe it in a sense. At some level of assent, it made sense to me that my existence was due to a God who would not abandon me to darkness, who wanted me to say yes to him. The alternative was even more insane. But if I stopped and let the reality of death sink in—prompted by a wait at a traffic light with a cemetery in sight or a glance at the obituary page—I was twelve again, and the darkness in there got very dark, indeed.

When that happened, I'd have to make a decision. Stay stuck or trust, work it out and pray through it? Yes, I believe in Jesus, I believe in the witness of the apostles, I believe it all happened and that Jesus lives. It worked, and I would be okay for a while after that. Until the next cemetery view I couldn't avoid because that light would just not change and let me move on.

I knew the way out. I could see it, point others to it. I could argue for it with conviction. But I couldn't ever get my whole self, body and soul and will, over to that place. I was still afraid.

～

Well, here we are at McDonald's, finally—about thirty minutes late, dashing my pride at being early, which we were when we hit the outskirts of Palermo—and there she is. Jacqueline is small and wiry, in her late thirties, holding a sign with our name on it as she stands in the parking lot. Katie shifts to the backseat with the little boys so our guide can slip into the front and show me the way out of here.

So that's how it's going to be? *I*—the tourist with three days' Sicilian driving experience and none of that except the last thirty minutes of it in a large city—*I* would be the one driving us through Palermo, up the narrow streets to Monreale? Really?

As I guide the car along the narrow city streets winding up to Monreale, Jacqueline tells me about her life, a precious gift that she obviously does not value as much as she should. She was born in California but has lived in Sicily, her father's homeland, for twenty years now. She twists in her seat and asks the children how they have enjoyed the trip so far, asks us what we thought about Scopello and Erice. When we pause in front of markets— which is often—she points out the various kinds of fish and other sea creatures, and she tells me about growing and preserving capers. Those two-foot long green things we're gaping at, hanging from the market awnings? Those are Sicilian zucchini, and the best part about them are the leaves, she says. They are fuzzy and delicious, those Sicilian zucchini leaves.

～

We didn't absolutely need a guide for Monreale. I could have arrived up here (eventually) without her help and found the parking lot outside the town walls. We didn't need a guide to walk with us past mosaic workshops and souvenir shops into the center of town to the piazza in front of the deceptively plain façade of the duomo. We could have found the door, paid the fee, and explored the church and the monastic cloister next door without help.

Sure, I could have hauled out the *Blue Guide* and pointed to floor and walls and read aloud about what surrounds us myself. But this spot was probably the most complex historical site we'd be touring, and one I had thought would be a key for any of us (including me) even beginning to appreciate the rich layers of Sicilian history—of Normans and Saracens, of Christians Latin and Eastern, of Muslims, all crowded here on this island. It would be worth it to pay someone who actually knew what she was talking about. Besides, experience has taught me that the chances of the guided actually listening to what is being said increase by a factor of ten if anyone—*anyone*—except me is doing the talking.

❧

Like so many churches I have encountered in Italy, the duomo's largely unadorned façade of reddish stone Romanesque towers that don't even match each other, and what strikes me as an afterthought of a white arched portico that clashes with both of them, barely hints at what's inside. As we step through the doors from the piazza, we all, including Jacqueline, cross ourselves with the holy water at the door; and although I have read about what we would see and had examined pictures, none of that really prepares me, because real life is more than pictures, is more than words on a page.

The interior is vast and every inch of it, floor to ceiling, is covered with mosaics set against gold. The gold—over two thousand kilograms of it was used by Byzantine craftsman brought from the east to do the job—glows or glimmers, depending on how the light strikes it. The mosaics tell stories, of course: patriarchs, prophets, apostles, and saints live out their journeys of call, rejection, discovery, and sacrifice across every level of the walls, on the ceiling, on columns, in every corner.

The guide points out details and tells stories. I'm particularly drawn by two points of artistry: the crafting of how the bodies and parts of bodies underwater appear; as well as the angels' wings, the angles and colors of which—muted brownish reds, whites, and edges of blue—remind me of patterns in Native American art.

Saints surround us. Saints who answered Jesus's call to sell everything, give the money to the poor and follow him, that enthralling invitation to give yourself over to the God who made himself powerless, an invitation to poverty embodied in precious stone because a man went all out to overwhelm another man with his power up here, on his very own royal mountain.

For that's why Monreale exists as an archdiocesan see, as the center of religious power it once was: a very worldly rivalry. In short, the twelfth-century Norman king William II stood in opposition to the Archbishop of Palermo and his alliances. His way of doing battle was to invite the Benedictines to Monreale—the "royal mountain"—to set up shop. Since the abbot of a monastery is the equivalent of a bishop, William then had his perfectly legal justification for the creation of an archdiocese, an alternative center of power looking, from a great height, down into Palermo and its outmaneuvered archbishop.

As is traditional when a patron builds a church, William is built into the mosaics, too, handing a model of his church to the Virgin. No Palermo archbishop writhes underneath his heel, but he might as well have, I'm thinking.

Above all that, above us all, Christ looks down from the great heights of the nave, above and behind the altar. The image is that of the traditional, Eastern Christian iconic image of Christ Pantocrator—Divine Ruler and Judge. He looms from the chest up, his robes are gold and royal blue, and his gaze is stern and steady, the seriousness not eased at all by the quirky-looking lock of hair falling in the middle of his forehead or the contours and wrinkles in face.

He looks out and down at us, travelers who in turn point up at him. We murmur to each other, squint and listen; we pick up some details but miss more because of the distance, the dim light, or because we just don't know what to look for.

And this is why I needed a guide, I see. No matter how much I had read, I wouldn't be able to make sense of this on my own. Without someone to help me figure it out, I would just be passing through. I needed someone who had been here before. I was glad for it.

We had been delayed a bit in entering the church because of a wedding being celebrated on this late Friday morning in June. The just-married couple make their way back down the center aisle, smiling, waving, receiving good wishes from tourists. Little girls stop in their tracks and stare, entranced. Bigger girls try not to be so obvious, but they watch too, and some of them remember.

Joseph and Michael make up a game as they skip along King William's complicated, intricate, expensive mosaic floor. The king's bones lie in a sarcophagus in a side area off the nave. The boys barely notice him as they race by, playing their mysterious private game, in a mad rush to see what's outside, what comes next.

On the Sunday after Mike died, on the day before his funeral Mass, I was driving from Gainesville to St. Augustine, where he would be buried, the little boys were in the backseat, and Katie was in the front reading aloud to me from the Gospel of Mark.

We were in Mike's car because it was the better one of the two of ours, more dependable than the ten-year-old SUV that I drove. How odd that the notice confirming that the debt on this car, his car, had been paid off arrived in the mail the day he died.

So we were driving the paid-for car through the flat, scrubby landscape of northeast Florida, mostly in silence, me worried and anxious about what was ahead of me. For this afternoon, I would see his body for the first time since last Tuesday and they would see his dead body for the first time, period. I was worried and I was scared for all of us, worried for the children, scared for myself because I just couldn't imagine how I could do this, what it would be like to see his dead body, sit with it—him—for four hours. I didn't want to go where I was going and do what I had to do for all the reasons you can imagine, but most of all because I didn't want him to be dead.

In the midst of this worried, sad silence, I spied a book on the ledge of the backseat. One of Mike's Bibles, stuck back there for who knows what reason. I told Joseph to grab it and give it to Katie, and without thinking about it much, I told her to start reading to me from the Gospel of Mark.

And so she did, her strong young voice, practiced in debate and theater, telling me about Jesus and what he did.

I stopped her after a couple of chapters and asked if she'd noticed a word that had popped up a lot. Because I'd noticed it.

She studied the pages.

"Immediately?"

A+.

Euthus it is in Greek. The Gospel of Mark is infused with this sense of urgency. *Immediately* he got up. *Immediately* they went out. *Immediately*.

And then . . . *immediately* the thought came to mind of how much this characterized Mike, who was absolutely all about *immediately*. He was the instigator, the motivator, the one who got everyone up and out and moving. . . . *Immediately*.

And yes, it was how he died, with barely an extra breath to spare. *Immediately*.

Katie kept reading, and people kept encountering Jesus and being healed and *immediately* he would go do something else for someone else and they would react with fear, with gratitude, only barely understanding what had happened to them, who he was before he moved on.

Tears came to my eyes, and for the first time in five days, the sorrow was mixed—just a little bit—with something else. It felt like gratitude, and that's what it was: gratitude. For Mike. That he had lived at all, even though he had died. Gratitude for what he'd brought into my life: humor and absurdity and two little boys, but what counted now was his nagging challenge to put God first—absolutely first—worship Christ, not other people's opinions, not your own weakness, not your own ego, not other human beings, friends or enemies. *God Alone* he tried to live by, he prayed for the grace to live by. *God Alone* I put on his Mass card. Jesus is Lord, not anyone else.

This hint of gratitude? That impulse to say *thank you*? Well, I pushed it aside. Quickly. It was too soon for anything but straight-up sorrow right now.

But Katie read on, and before I knew it, Mark took me to the country of the Gerasenes where a possessed man lived chained among the tombs, and lived in that place because he was as good as dead.

Jesus drives the demons out of this man. The neighbors, upon seeing the now free man healed and clean, turn to Jesus and demand something of him. Not to be healed themselves, mind you. No, they insist that he leave.

Immediately. God Alone. Leave us.

Just like that, my life, Mike's life, Mike's body lying at the end of this road, and Jesus all fell together and we were all right there amid the tombs. I had sensed that tiny buzz of grace when I considered *immediately* and all it conveyed, and I had resisted. I could keep that up if I wanted. I could certainly say, "Leave me." It was up to me.

My daughter read more of Mark, the road stretched on, I studied our little boys reflected in the rearview mirror, and I kept driving to the place I had to take us all that day.

A few hours later, we were there. In a daze, I stood with his mother and sisters, waiting for the man in charge to open the door, listening to his soothing, practiced voice, explaining things. I'd thought what I was about to do was impossible and undoable, mostly because I never really imagined it could happen and also because I had lived so petrified of death for so long. Now I was coming face-to-face with it, on my husband's face, and this time, I couldn't hang at the door and slump against any walls. I would have to go in, walk up close, and see.

But then the man opened the door and it was almost as if I was propelled forward. I didn't hold back as I thought I would. I almost ran. I dropped the framed pictures I was carrying. I rushed up to the casket. I hadn't seen him in so long.

I stopped and as I stared at him, the Gospel I had picked for Mass blasted through my soul: *Why do you look for the living among the dead?*

I saw his body lying there and while it echoed his presence, it just wasn't him. I turned to his poor mother and I whispered that. "It isn't him," I said, which I doubt helped her one bit, but it was true. I cried, but I'll tell you the truth, out of the hundred reasons I cried when I saw him there, one of them was relief.

All I can do is tell you what I felt at that moment. I felt that he had gone ahead, had cut through the layers of ambiguity and paradox, of irony, of confusion and darkness, and even though it looked like he was lying there perfectly still, he was actually moving, pointing, just like he always had, telling me *God Alone*, and this cold heaviness was not the end. He had gone ahead, and because he'd done this first, I knew I could go too.

And just like that, standing there, I wasn't afraid, not for him, and for the first time ever in my entire life—I wasn't afraid for myself, either.

The fear was just—gone.

Euthus.

9

Lovely little Monreale on the hill, you certainly deserve more than three hours of our time, and we would really love to give it to you, but really, what are we supposed to do with ourselves during your nap? Wander empty streets, study the ceramic bowls, mosaic miniatures, and Pinocchio puppets arrayed behind windows of closed shops, then sit in the hot sun on the steps of closed churches for the next couple of hours until you wake up again?

This is my first serious encounter with the reposa here in Sicily, and sorry for the cliché, but my jaw really does drop when Jacqueline tells me, after she has pointed us to a good restaurant for lunch, that the afternoon rest lasts here, not until three, as I had experienced in Rome, but until four o'clock.

"Or four thirty." She shrugs before she rushes to catch a bus back down the hill to Palermo.

Well. We're standing behind the duomo, where she has brought us, not only to start us down the correct alleyway to the restaurant, but also to show us the fascinating back end of the cathedral, a dizzying, clearly Arabic-styled array of tiles arranged in overlapping arches and flowering patterns, reaching far into the sky. Another marvelous piece of the multicultural puzzle here in Monreale, but not enough to occupy us—or even me by myself—for two hours once lunch is finished. And no, lingering over a leisurely lunch for the afternoon is not an option when half of your party is composed of little boys under nine years old.

There's one type of establishment that just might still be open,

I suspect, and as we turn a corner on our way back to the car from the duomo piazza, I see that I'm right. Do gelateria ever close?

The boys ponder their options, which doesn't take long since they resolutely refuse to move beyond vanilla or chocolate. Katie casts a much wider net, usually leaning a fruity direction and, of course, Nutella. I study the brioche piled in a basket on top of the glass case, and a light goes on. I had read that Sicilians will sometimes have gelato for breakfast, scoops of it wedged in rolls. In reading about this, I couldn't picture it, since when I thought of "rolls," I was imagining small little palm-sized bites, but now, seeing the brioche that you almost need two hands to grab, I get it, and point it out to Katie. A light goes on for her, too, and later, on a bench back in front of the duomo, as she takes the last bite, she declares that this is the way she wants to eat gelato from now on for the rest of the trip.

It's like a cream donut, except it's bigger, colder, drippier, and better. And it lives here, in Sicily.

Late afternoon, on the autostrada heading south of Palermo, the boys and Katie are dozing, and I'm thinking about how much I'd worried about this, about driving in Sicily. Looking back, the stress seems not only pointless but borderline insane. I'm thinking that not only is it manageable, but that I like it a lot, and that Sicilian driving and I might actually be on the same wavelength. I'm really not sure what that says about me.

The basic idea—besides *keep moving* or *you're in a car . . . so drive it already!*—seems to be that rules, such as they are, exist to serve people, not people the rules. Someone else once said something along those same lines, as I recall.

So when I think of American traffic, my sense memory is dominated by sitting, but aching to move on. Waiting, even at a red light at midnight, with not another soul around, which is what we Americans tend to do. Flow is what I'm feeling on the road in Sicily, here on the autostrada, naturally, but even in the middle of Palermo or when I drive through small towns: a dynamic in which the slower drivers know to make way for the faster ones, moving to the right to let another car pass, onto the shoulder if necessary if there's no passing lane, a scene in which the roundabout replaces the hard angles of the intersection. You slow down, but you never really seem to actually *stop*.

The roundabout has become of my favorite parts of driving in Sicily. It sounds crazy, but I sort of *love* the roundabouts, which are more common than traffic lights in cities and are standard at intersections outside of them. You merge, you peel off, and the really great thing is that if you miss your turnoff, you just circle again and catch it next time.

It's a forgiving way of getting from one place to another, with more space to figure things out, pull aside, and slow down a bit as you correct your mistakes, all of which is a good thing for people like me, who often have no clue where they're going at all.

Right now, however, I do have a clue. I'm taking us to the agriturismo—the working farm set up to receive tourists—for a week. I had spent so much time researching this part of the trip that I could probably sketch out a fairly accurate map of Sicilian agriturismos freehand, without any references. It was ridiculous, but it became an interesting problem to me, a puzzle, for selecting our lodgings for that week turned out to be about more than what the food would be like, what animals might be around for the children to enjoy, location, or price. I would study the websites, alternating between imaginative flights about dinner *al fresco* in the country and frozen indecision.

Where, I kept wondering, am I *supposed* to be for that week? What will I miss if I pick the one outside of Catania over the one with the donkey in the south? Are there any wrong turns here, or will any choice give us great memories? Finally, I came to this one, this spot on a hill in the middle of Sicily, an organic farm that produces almonds, chickpeas, and olive oil from their own olives. What I saw in the photographs appealed to me because I could see myself there in a way that I couldn't in the others. The photos showed low-slung pinkish-pastel-looking buildings with tile roofs set on hills, surrounded by groves and vineyards that suggested expansiveness to me. I could see chairs scattered outdoors, next to a swimming pool, on a patio next to the house. It seemed to me that if I sat in one of those chairs, I would be very close to the pale blue sky. It looked as if there might be nothing in between me and that sky, at all.

~

What they say—they *all* say—is that the practical business of death overwhelms the emotions for a while and delays the confrontation with the truth of loss. It's true. Planning a funeral, adapting finances, changing your schedule, signing papers, and dealing with death certificates keeps you occupied.

But eventually the hours of the day empty and slow, there are no more distractions or excuses, and you have time to remember.

Ash Wednesday came on February 25 that year, three weeks after Mike died.

I went to get the mail that day after I returned from noon Mass. I was thinking about various Ash Wednesdays in the past, most of all about one Ash Wednesday night ages ago in Florida. We had agreed to go to an Eagles concert in Tampa with our friends Brian and Kathryn, not realizing when we set it up that it would fall on Ash Wednesday. Well, we went, but we were sort of embarrassed and abashed about going, and almost every Ash Wednesday since, Mike and I would remember and laugh about that night, about standing there outside the arena, watching a succession of tall, skinny girls in glittery strapless microminis tumble out of limos, a surprising number of them bearing dusty crosses on their foreheads.

So I sat in the car before I got out to grab the mail from the boxes near the apartment manager's office on that first day of

Lent, mourning. Mourning a dead husband, plagued with *what-ifs*, mourning that shared history that was now dust, thinking about the words murmured by the priest as he had traced ashes on my own forehead telling me that I, too, was dust and that I would return there.

Up to that point, for three weeks, every day's mail had been stacked high with condolence cards. Prayer cards, Mass cards, thoughtful letters from friends, even from strangers. Every day, the mailbox was crowded with sympathy.

I unlocked the mailbox on that Ash Wednesday afternoon and glanced through what was there. First I noticed what wasn't. There wasn't a card of any sort in the stack. It was the first day since I'd returned from burying him that I hadn't received even one condolence card.

The mailbox was still full, though. Full of bills. Every single piece of mail that day was a bill. Nothing extreme or delinquent, just the ordinary bills of this ordinary life. Lent was beginning and dust was settling. They told me that resurrection was coming, but that all seemed very far away that day as I tossed the notices of what I owed in the front seat and drove up to the quiet apartment, alone.

⌒

We've just passed Caltanissetta, so I rouse everyone and engage Katie to navigate. She's balancing the trip bible with a couple of maps printed out from the Internet, as well as my big map of Sicily, which I repeatedly hand to her, grab away, refold, and hand back, tapping at the point where I think we are and where we're going. Despite all of this and despite the fact that I really thought I knew where I was going this time, I naturally take the wrong exit and must backtrack. Once we get back to what I'm pretty sure is the right place this time, we're bumping along on a dirt road cutting through vineyards. We could reach out and pick the purple grapes, hanging heavy on the vines, so close to our open windows.

We end up in front of a locked gate at the bottom of a hill, and I decide that this must be it. I had been told to call when we arrive, and I have a phone that purportedly works in this country, and I did converse with the tour guide on it yesterday, but it's confounding me now. I can't get through—the problem is that I am never sure where the phone thinks I am calling from. Does it think I'm calling from Sicily or Birmingham? Do I need to enter the country code or not? I can't reach Claudia, the farm's owner, so finally I resort to the ridiculous: we take out the laptop, find, miraculously, that we can connect, and there, sitting at the gate to her property, olive trees on my left, vineyards behind me, and wheat fields on my right—and Claudia herself a few hundred meters away—I send her an e-mail.

~

Thanks to technology, I could see and hear Mike after he died whenever I wanted to, if I wanted to. We didn't own a video camera, but I had photographs, of course, and also his voice: on archived radio programs, on CDs of retreat and mission talks.

I am of two minds about the lack of videos. On the one hand, I'm sorry I don't have any moving pictures of him alive, laughing, talking, and breathing. But on the other hand, I'm not. I don't know if I could even bear to watch them, for I was torn up enough about just listening to his voice alone. It even took me a while to decide where I stood and what I would do about that—his deep, resonant voice just a click away. I didn't want to descend into fantasy, trying to pretend that he was really still around. I had no idea whether hearing him again would comfort me or slice off yet another sliver of my heart.

One night in the middle of that first Lent, I ached so much for his voice that the decision was made for me. I had to hear him again. I lay in bed, opened the computer up, found the website of the Catholic radio station with its several archived interviews. I stared at his photograph on the web page, read their words *Rest in*

Peace below that picture, and clicked on the link. The interviewer spoke first, so I had time to brace myself, but it wasn't enough time. He still took my breath away when he started to speak.

It was Lent now, as I was doing that, and this was Lenten stuff he was talking about, and so of course he was talking about God Alone, about suffering, about the necessity and inevitability of it, and once again, returning to his favorite subject of God Alone, about not relying on the things or people of this world for our happiness.

Because that's what he always said when I raised it, when I looked to him for reassurance about happiness. I would do that whiny thing and I would ask him, *Do I make you happy?*, and he would sigh and say that he would be in bad shape indeed if his happiness depended on my existence. Not because he wasn't happy now, but because he needed to be "happy"—at peace— whether I was around or not, no matter if he liked his job or not, or whatever was going on or whoever was around him. He'd make his case as he always did that our happiness shouldn't depend on anything except God. *I should be able to be happy*, he'd say, *even if you died tomorrow.* He'd take his eyes off the television and look at me.

And so should you.

This is the kind of thing he was talking about in the interview, and as I listened, I marveled that there was actually a time, not too long ago, when that voice echoed in this room for real, laughing, comforting, arguing. I almost couldn't believe it. Had such a time really been? That he was here, with me, us? I lasted for ten minutes, but it was too much to bear, to listen to his voice nagging me about finding peace that endures.

All right, I thought as I slammed the laptop shut. *I get it. You win. God Alone. Argument over. I've learned my lesson.*

You can come back now.

❧

We watch a cloud of dust descending from the hill on the other side of the gate. A small station wagon emerges from the cloud and stops, a woman jumps out of the driver's side, unlocks the gate, and swings it wide open. I recognize her from the website photos, and she introduces herself as Claudia, the owner. She's just a bit older than I with short, tousled dark hair and a broad smile. We exchange *Ciao*s all around, Michael's hair gets tousled, and as she locks the gate back up she tells me that no, she hadn't read my e-mail, but her husband working in Caltanissetta had. He'd called her right away to let her know we were here.

We all get back in our cars, we follow her up the hill, and she shows us our home for the next week. The stucco house is painted pale pink and has a tile roof. The family—Claudia, Marco, and their teenaged daughter—live in the house proper, and a small block of two apartments and two rooms has been built on to the side for guests like us. Our apartment has two bedrooms—one with twin beds for Katie and Joseph—and the other with a double for me and Michael. We've got a small kitchen and living room, and a table spread with all kinds of travel literature; we've got a new, shiny bathroom, and it all opens out onto a tiled patio there on top of the hill, with huge rosemary bushes right outside the door, a covered area with chairs, hammocks, tables, and Ping-Pong and a swimming pool.

Which is all very nice, but I can immediately tell what will push the farm up from almost "ideal" to the level you might call "paradise." They have four legs, there are two of them—one is white, the other is beige—and this is going to be the best week ever because there are dogs.

As she explains the stove and the bathrooms to me, Claudia alludes to other guests. A young British couple is staying here—they are visiting Mount Etna today and will return later tonight and will be leaving tomorrow after a morning's lesson in making Sicilian pizza. I file it as evidence that a day trip to the promised volcano will indeed be doable from here. They're in one of the rooms upstairs. In the apartment next to ours are Americans, and we meet them soon after we arrive, as we gather in the common room for predinner drinks, cheese, almonds, and olives grown here on the farm.

The woman—a nurse here from San Diego with her twentysomething niece—is about my age. She is thin and small with lots of dark hair on her head that pours down her back. She's a vegetarian, very deliberate in her speech, intentional in her gaze, generally intense, and has very big teeth. The niece works with the Peace Corp in an eastern European country and is larger, heavier, and of a clearly mordant temperament, balancing out her aunt's enthusiasm.

They are, like most Americans I will meet here in Sicily, on a family quest, tracing their own singular trail of one of the millions trod by Sicilians who emigrated to the States a hundred years ago—one-fourth of the population of the island left the hopeless impoverishment for the United States and Australia during that period. These two wandering Americans on a mission have no car, though, and this is a farm in the middle of farmland, a.k.a., the country, with no bus stop at the corner. I cannot quite figure out how they are planning to get around to search out the church registries and find the villages where their grandparents and great-aunts were born and lived. Should I be ashamed to admit that as they tell me this at dinner, I am very glad that my car is a small one? Probably.

Having unpacked and explored a bit, we gather for dinner. Marco is in from his medical practice in town; their daughter, who speaks English and is on Facebook, comes down; and then there are all of us Americans. The British couple has not yet returned from Mount Etna, of course, but they will be here later. Claudia speaks the best English, although Marco can manage.

The dinner is bountiful. There's salad, pasta with pesto that Joseph, my pickiest eater, devours—another testament to the value of starving a child for eight hours between meals. There are other vegetables—including sautéed zucchini leaves—some sort of scallopini and bread. Once again, I wonder how they eat like this and don't all weigh a thousand pounds. They actually must not eat like this all the time—that's the only answer to the puzzle. They can't. Who could?

After dinner, the other Americans retire to their apartment, but we spread out on the covered patio as the sun sinks into shadows tinged with purples and pinks. The boys discover Ping-Pong paddles and attempt to play, but they have the most fun when the dogs give chase to an errant ball, which happens approximately every seventeen seconds. Katie occasionally joins in their game, but mostly she burrows deep in a hammock chair, letting it envelop and cocoon her as she reads Camus.

Me, I watch them, fiddle with the settings on my camera, try to figure out how to take good pictures in the fading light, and write things. I look up from my journal, catch a scent of rosemary, and see white pinpoints of light begin to appear spread above me; I can't believe that I'm really here on a Sicilian farm. I feel, not just as if I have stopped at a point on a journey, but that I have arrived at some sort of destination.

The boys play, hardly ever hitting the little white ball. The dogs trot over, chase the balls, and nose the delighted boys. Michael and Joseph pile on Katie in the hammock chair and they're all suspended there crowded together, swinging and giggling, demanding that I spin them all around, again and again.

It's good to be here. My guilt about the cost and the privilege, and my survivor's guilt, seem to fade with the light. They might be back again tomorrow, along with the sun. They probably will. But right now, I'll let it be a good thing to be here. No matter how we got here, no matter why. I'll try to be happy. Knowing that it could all disappear tomorrow, knowing that everything could change in a moment.

10

I WAKE UP SATURDAY MORNING THINKING ABOUT MIKE, but what's new about that? Sicily, Alabama, it's all the same. At home in our bedroom, empty space beside me, or here, the warm sun awakening me through the eastward-looking open window, his younger son sprawled, abandoned to temporary sleep beside me, it doesn't matter. Barely five months after he died, he's last on my mind at night and is still there in the morning, first thing, when I awake.

But in between, he disappears.

I've not dreamed of him once since he died. His sisters do. His youngest sister told me that in her regular dreams of her brother, what is usually happening in one setting or another is that she is telling him—almost trying to convince him—that he is dead.

On hearing this, I can't help but move into Mike's mental space and tell her what I think he would say. His favored school of dream interpretation insisted that every character in a dream is simply a dimension of the dreamer's self. So in her dreams, she's really just trying to convince herself that he really is gone.

⁓

To make sure I remember is why I think about him then, before I rise to confront the day without him. I have to remember two things: to remember what he was like when he was alive, and to remember that he died.

I think about him alive—mostly his eyes, for that was one of his most striking features, not for their grayish-green color, but for the size of them. Michael has the same huge eyes, and strangers comment on them. And then they rub his head.

So I remember those open eyes, and then I force myself back to my place beside his casket in the funeral home in St. Augustine. *That happened.* I have to force myself to admit it. *That happened. They sewed his eyes shut.*

I remember this, too: he didn't really look like himself in there.

Johnette, one of his authors from his time in publishing, missed the viewing, but made it to the funeral on Monday. Her husband had died two years before. I told her that it had not looked like him, and it was something about the mouth, especially, that was so wrong, almost twisted, drawn down. She nodded. She had been at her husband's side when he died of cancer and was confident that in his casket, just a couple of days later, he would surely look like himself. He didn't.

It's always the mouth, she said. *They never get the mouth right.*

Mike's hair drove him crazy. It was thin and never did what he wanted. Joseph? He has that hair. Mike had a couple of cowlicks. Joseph's got them, too, in the same spots on his own head. Lying there in the casket, Mike's body speaking to me of both presence and absence, one thing was right amid everything else that was so wrong. Just as it did when he was alive, one lock of hair stood straight up.

My friend Dorothy and I murmured, at almost the same time, as we stood there and looked at him, *You'd think that they could have fixed that,* and she gently tried to make the hair lay flat. I couldn't do it myself, couldn't bring myself to touch his head. Partly because I had been warned not to, because it would feel so shockingly different from what my habit of touching him alive would lead me to expect. But partly because it was okay with me if that hair stood straight up, just as it was, just as it was when he was.

～

Why do I seek the living among the dead? Well, where else am
I supposed to look? This ritual of thinking about Mike alive and
then dead, which I do every morning and every evening as I try
to fall asleep is me trying to figure out reality, which now includes another dimension, in a way I can't deny. It doesn't seem
to work, though, this studying him dead and alive in my mind's
eye, so I give up every time and hand it over to God, which is
probably what I'm supposed to do, but even then I can't set it
aside completely. For during the day, I still walk around, seeing
things, doing things, and this whole business of Mike here one
day, warm flesh and huge open eyes and deep laugh, and then
gone the next, cold flesh, closed eyes and silent, underground,
is simply not computing. I keep asking where he went—I can't
stop—because it just seems impossible and too bizarre.

If I broke a plate, I could look down on the ground and see
all the pieces on the floor. Broken, even smashed into a pile of
ceramic dust, nothing that physically constituted the plate would
be missing. If you had enough glue and finely tuned tweezers,
you could piece the plate back together and recognize it for what
it was. It would still be that particular plate, only broken and put
back together.

But him? His body was there in one piece, more or less, minus
his fluids. His body lying in that casket isn't missing anything on
the surface, but he's still gone. There he is, with that lock of hair
sticking up like it always did, but I still can't see him.

Where did he go?

A few weeks after Sicily, on the beach in Florida, little Michael
will toss this off, skipping ahead of me in the sand:

"Sometimes Daddy comes to me in my dreams," he says.

Lucky, I think. Then carefully, gently, so as not to pose a leading question or put pressure, I ask a question, because I happen to
believe that there's more to dreams than us talking to ourselves.

"Does Daddy talk to you in your dreams? Does he say anything?"

"Yes."

I catch my breath again and hold it.

"What does he say?"

"I don't remember." He shrugs, and skips away, down to the water gently lapping the shore.

～

This Saturday morning in Sicily, I lie in bed watching the sun rise higher in the sky, thinking about him, because I always do. Michael shifts, still sleeping, turns away from the growing light, and as he buries his face in his pillow, he sighs.

～

A little after eight, the boys and I make it to the common area for breakfast, while Katie sleeps on. The food is laid out on the long table where we ate last night, a great spread with more protein than we saw in Scopello, hard-boiled eggs—which Joseph eats, but only the whites—and some cold meat. Claudia finds us there and encourages us to take some of everything, some of the yogurt, the fruit, the cheese, the sweet breakfast bread, and—we don't even have to ask—cold milk. The boys like it, of course, but breakfast is nothing compared to who's waiting outside, so as soon as they feel even a little full, they're done and out, racing around the top of this hill with the dogs.

Claudia and I talk about the farm and about the midsized town of Caltanissetta just a few kilometers north. In exploring the question of Sunday Mass before we came, I had discovered that there is a Poor Clares' monastery in the town, and it seemed like it would be good to worship with the sisters living in the footsteps of Francis and Clare.

Perhaps I shouldn't be surprised, but I am when Claudia tells me that she knows the monastery well: she is friends with some of the sisters and has helped them with their gardens. She declares that she and Marco will accompany us to Mass there, tomorrow morning at ten.

Claudia also convinces me that Agrigento is not too far for a day trip today. Agrigento is the site of a collection of temples built by the Greeks in the sixth and fifth centuries before Christ, and purportedly some of the finest of this sort of thing outside of Greece itself. I knew it wasn't a great distance, but I had dithered about doing any kind of travel off the farm on our first day here. She convinces me that it would be worth it today, that the route is almost all highway; and, in answer to my query about grocery stores, she tells me that there is a Carrefour on the way.

～

Carrefour is the Walmart of Europe, and a stop on the way to Agrigento should meet some immediate needs like sunscreen, bottled water, lotion for some almost-burned patches of skin, and, of course, snacks. Always snacks. Joseph's little game system also needs a converter for the charger. Since Claudia says that Carrefour has everything we could possibly need, we'll stop there on the way back for food for dinner, too. The farm is not exactly like the B and B in Scopello in that dinner is not served every night. When it is, I'm not sure, and since Claudia specifically says we could get food for our dinners at Carrefour, I'm taking that as a hint that she and her kitchen assistant won't be cooking tonight.

Katie, roused and showered and refreshed, joins us. We say farewell to the dogs for now, bump over dirt roads to the highway, and after about ten minutes, we're pulling off the road, heading to what looks like an enormous, windowless warehouse sitting on a rise. Most of the parking is underneath the functional-looking structure, which we assume houses only the Carrefour and wine store listed on the small sign outside. Like yesterday in Monreale, the relatively stark exterior of the most dominating building around reveals nothing about this church, this cathedral.

The wide escalator—a flat, moving ramp with no steps, to accommodate shopping carts—carries us from the dimness below up into a bright, busy space—it's really a mall—and we are met, first thing, by the glittering storefront of a Swarovski crystal store. But even better, as delighted as anyone being surprised by the finest mosaic detail in the duomo, pilgrims alert me to an astonishing surprise:

"MOM! It's a Game Stop!"

Before we tackle that issue, we enter Carrefour, which lies straight ahead and is set up just like the superhuge megamarts at home—household items, clothing and electronics and such, on one side and groceries on the other. We wander, taking in the differences and similarities. Colored pencils seem like they might be a good idea, so we grab a pack. Plastic cups. Sunscreen. Lotion, since some of us are already close to burned. We buy crackers that seem like they might be similar to Wheat Thins. The boys delight in the sweets, and there are a lot because Europeans love their sweets, especially chocolate—later, in Barcelona, when we're looking for dry cereal, it will be a challenge to find one that *isn't* chocolate in some form or another. We wander the food aisles, making notes of what we will buy on our return trip. We look at the fish, the octopus, two small rays laid out on the ice, just chilling.

I feel abashed that I am here in Sicily, land of the picturesque, and I'm essentially shopping in Walmart instead of a picturesque store in a picturesque hill town with old ladies dressed in black, all of us carrying our net shopping bags, being picturesque.

But of course, this place called Sicily is a real place where people live and work in the twenty-first century, and not Epcot Sicily constructed with my fantasies, no matter how picturesque, as the template. These locals probably rejoiced at the opening of their very own big box store. Someone told me later that since Carrefour is in fact competing with those venerable little traditional shops, the quality of their food is actually quite high—it has to be.

The young woman who checks us out isn't friendly—they

hardly ever are in Italy, I've found. You'd think they would have reason to be nicer than they are since European store clerks generally do business from the comfort of stools—a practice that makes the lot of American cashiers, standing for hours as they scan and make change—seem unreasonable and almost bizarre to me.

But even from the relative comfort of her seat, my cashier today makes no effort to hide her irritation at me, for I have committed the mortal sin of Not Having Exact Change. This is to be expected, for Italian shopkeepers are known for despising anything except exact change, and if you are a hapless tourist (check) who has just retrieved your euros in twenties or (worse) fifties from the ATM (check) and you really had no choice, God help you and watch out.

In regard to the most important mission of the morning, though, there is no adapter or converter at Carrefour, and neither is there one at "Eurotronics" next door. Or Game Stop, for that matter. The fellow who helps me at Eurotronics understands what I need without either of us speaking each other's language, and he points to "Brico" on the other side of Carrefour—a hardware store of a sort. Six women in red smocks standing around in this Brico place listen to me and watch my hand motions, then all shrug in a mix of incomprehension and indifference before a young fellow grasps the point immediately.

"American to Italian or Italian to American?" he asks, briskly leading me to the back of the store. I tell him and he digs it out of a bin, and I pay the two euros. I worry because it's an adapter, not a converter, and it's my impression that my equipment will immediately explode with just an adapter. We'll see. That DS is a mixed blessing, anyway.

Joseph is quite relieved when he sees what I've found for him. Pokémon lives.

(We hope.)

Well, I think as we ride down the escalator to the car and I zip my wallet shut, *at least now I have some change. Maybe the next cashier will like me.*

⌒

Back in Alabama, there are no Carrefours, of course, and since I'll always take Target over Walmart, I must consider myself fortunate because there's one near our apartment. It's big and clean and bright and very Targety. You know. Not as utilitarian as Walmart, crisper and uncluttered, that bright red always lurking in your peripheral vision in that Targety way.

There was a time, not too long ago, in which a last-minute request or a late discovery of a missing staple would send me right over the edge. But in those first months after Mike died, my position shifted on that issue. It was more like, "You need a compass? I'll just go to Target." "Oh look, only half a gallon of milk left. I guess I need to go to Target." And of course, the one we all know and hate most of all, "Poster board? No problem! I'll just run to Target. Be back in a minute."

So in the dusk, I very willingly got in my car alone and started the short drive that took me between a river and a large, abandoned hospital, to Target, to get whatever they'd discovered they'd need, to pick up something I'd just discovered I really, really needed, and needed tonight. That night. *Now.* Gotta go.

If you'd seen me there at Target, though, and if you looked closely, you might have noticed that my eyes seemed red and my breathing was uneven. You might have even suspected I was avoiding you before you finally stopped me in front of the poster boards or the bread. Well, you did see right. They were (red) and I was (avoiding you) because after being around others all day, having to hold up my end and theirs, and still living in the midst of his things, pondering what to do with it all, at the end of a day like that—maybe it was the day all the death certificates came in the mail—a thick envelope holding all ten copies because, you know, they tell you that you will need to prove to a lot of people that he's dead—after all that I might have practically run to the car the minute I was able so that on the way to Target, the dam could just burst.

How many people begged Jesus to help them see? I'm one of them now. Well, I always was, with my blind spots and my doubts, but now I'm all in with blind beggars on the road, in villages. I'm also in with my two favorite blind guys that Jesus meets. The first, Jesus has to touch twice because after the first time, he could see a bit, but not perfectly. Not right away. The second one whose story I revisit again and again is given all his sight back immediately, but what fascinates me is how long it takes him to figure out who did this to him and why. He only comes to the answer—that Jesus, the Lord, has given him sight—after being questioned about it, repeatedly. At first he answers that the one who did it was "man," but eventually, as he has to answer question after question, he recognizes Jesus for who he really is. He sees.

I'd like to see. I'd like to see Mike; I'd like to see what this is all about, this life, death and eternity. I'd also like to not have to wait to see *all of this*. Paul tells me that someday I will, indeed, see it "face-to-face," which is great but still leaves me confused as to what the point of waiting is.

I would also like to not have to work at this, to not have to puzzle every night at the apparent chasm between the laughter and the silence, the confounding difference between eyes closed for a Saturday afternoon nap and eyes sewn shut.

I'm stuck here, now, never dreaming of him, but seeing him, studying him dead and alive for clues behind my closed eyes. I want to see more and I want to see it now, but too bad. I have to stay right here, working my way through the dark to Target, where the lights are very bright, but somehow, I still can't seem to see.

11

S O THIS IS LIFE IN THE RUINS.
You pick your way through rubble, trace ancient paths. You stand among structures that bustled with importance once, but no longer, that serve no purpose except as set decoration to stand against a light blue sky and loom above a brilliant blue sea, past glories collapsed, past dreams drained away, past certainties trampled by barely comprehending travelers.

It's hot in the Valley of the Temples this afternoon. A shirtless old man passes me on a path. I am going up to the Temple of Concord, he is coming down from it. His mustache is white, as is the hair on his head, hair that reaches to his neck, slicked back with either sweat or some oily product. He is shirtless, his bare chest and generous gut are red and glistening, and he walks briskly down the hill, pushing a baby stroller. An empty baby stroller. I file the image so I can tell Mike, but of course immediately remember that I can't. The lag time between the reflexive . . . *Mike will love this* . . . and the realization . . . *he's dead* . . . is shorter now. Infinitesimal. But it's still there. A habit, a tic, a wish. But it's still where I live, here in the shadow of useless old thoughts with nowhere to go.

～

Just about twenty minutes after we leave Carrefour, we see the city of Agrigento, the region's capital, tumbling down a hill ahead, in between us and the sea. It's a haphazard mass of ochre, pink, beige, and yellow structures crowding and jostling up against one another, packed tightly on that hill. We don't have to go up into the city to get to the Valley of the Temples, but head around it on the south.

The parking lot at the site is small, dusty, and quite full. There are lots of tourists here today, the most of our own kind we've encountered so far. After we park, we're immediately approached with offers of guided tours by guys in golf carts. We'll be doing this on our own today, so I wave them off and head to buy our tickets to the site. The attendant asks me what country we're from. I answer without thinking, see the woman behind the window frown slightly, and realize that I had totally forgotten about the ticket-buying secret handshake: that you always answer "Canadian," not because they won't let you in if you're American, but because Canadians get a discount that we, for some reason, don't.

⌒

We walk across the road, present our tickets at the gate, and start climbing the rising paths that will take us to the various temples and other structures that dot these hills. When we reach the Temple of Concord, we're struck by how complete it is. It barely seems to earn the name "ruin." It's beautiful, and almost glows, the sandstone of its columns burnished by centuries to a brownish orange. It's roped off, so we can't, of course, go inside to check it out, which disappoints the boys, even as they understand the fragility of these ancient, collapsing things. We can, though, stand here for a bit and consider the horizon, can once again try to see Africa; the boys can ask again if we can go there, and I can try to see whatever other things I'm always trying to see.

It occurs to me as I stand there, wrestling again with the mystery of what I can and can't see, trying to apprehend the continued being-in-not-here-anymore, that the mysteries of the invisible God's being and identity have never confounded me in the gut-wrenching way that the mystery of Mike-alive and then Mike-in-the-casket have. I've accepted those mysteries and even argued for their value as such. How, I would ask my skeptical, cynical students, could God be God if we could totally understand him? And look, I would point out, projecting certainty, how well do you even understand yourself? So why do you hold up mystery as evidence that God must not be? Isn't it the opposite?

Isn't it?

Up here, old temple columns built by the dead standing tall at my side, the living world spread out all around, I can see at least one thing clearly: I can see my own unseeing for what it is—a fact.

~

We wander back down the hill to some catacombs. Tombs. They're built into the side of a hill, and they are not sideways like caves, but just holes in the ground that look a lot like cisterns to me. The boys pick their way among the holes that probably descend ten feet or more. They walk in circles, balancing on the rims of these deep, narrow holes, and I am nervous about what they're doing, but they are not a bit scared. They teeter on the edge of the empty tombs, and it doesn't occur to them that they might be swallowed up. They're not afraid of falling into those tombs.

~

Walking away from the empty catacombs up toward more temples, we find ourselves at the tail end of an American tour group. A fellow in the back is loudly joking, obviously reveling in his role as Tour Comic. We pass a plaque placed by a CLUB UNESCO—a local group dedicated to the ideals of the United Nations cultural body. The Comedian riffs. "Hey, look, there used to be a club here!" he chortles. Loudly. "'Club UNESCO!' I'll have a beer—watch out where you piss—I ain't bullshitting you!" he goes on and on with my little boys in plain sight and hearing.

I turn to Katie and mutter, "Imagine being in a tour group with *him*."

Another man walking a step ahead of us, turns around, looks straight at me, and sighs as he says, "It's been *ten days*!"

Awkward! Well, I wasn't whispering, and I probably was indeed dancing on the edge of passive-aggressiveness, but I'm mortified anyway. The second fellow just laughs and tells us that they are part of a Catholic parish from West Virginia visiting here as—of course—an exploration of the members' Sicilian roots. It also turns out the man talking to us is named Michael, and he's on the tour with his brother, who is named Joseph.

We're amused at the coincidence, of the chances of two sets of American brothers, both named Michael and Joseph, meeting amid the Greek ruins in Sicily. We take photos. They take photos. There are jokes about being brothers. I see us all and where we will be thirty or forty years from now, and in response to the vision, I pray and resolve to do what I can to help my set of brothers stay close to each other since that time when all they will have, along with their half-siblings, is each other is coming. As I've learned, I can't predict when that time will come, and as I've also learned, I can't stop it, either.

～

We've followed the path from the Temple of Concord down past the catacombs and now we are back up on another hill, amid another temple, the Temple of Hercules, but this one is free for climbing because it's totally collapsed, spread out on the hill. This means it is practically paradise for the boys, who waste no time in conquest of these great ribbed stumps of stone. They're Indiana Jones, exploring, fighting, adventuring. They find nooks and crannies and shade, and then they leap out again, and stand atop the jumble of broken pieces, now one of the brothers victorious, now the other.

Katie and I sit and look around and read up some more on the history and try to take it in, maybe even retain some of it. Yes, basically this trip is about going places where Katie and I can eat and absorb a little history, and the boys can run around like madmen, and I can contemplate variations of *sic transit gloria mundi*—the inevitable passage of all earthly things, no matter how beautiful—for three weeks straight.

Now Michael and Joseph are no longer enemies, but are on the same team, in the same army. They're scrambling all over these ruined chunks of the Temple of Hercules and could probably keep it up for hours. They stand atop the safest high spot, they reach to the sky, they hide together in caves made of jumbled, fallen stones, and they are always victorious, no matter what. They conquer their foes, every time, together, on the same side, at least for today.

~

There are lots of bad moments when someone you love dies. You discover another scrap of paper in his handwriting, you live through his birthday, you realize you never paid the bill for his headstone, even though you could have sworn you did. But no. Too many tiny wounds a day to count, really, but the things is, the worst is never anything you expect. Just when you think you're doing okay, when you're on a good road and not feeling too terrible, it hits again.

I did a lot of hard things in those first weeks and months, did things that grieved me—picked out clothes for Mike to wear in his casket, gave away most of the rest. Sorted through his personal items, considered what I should keep for myself, but mostly for his sons.

I opened a box, about a week after he died on the treadmill, running, of something he'd ordered from Amazon. I was in his office, going through deliveries that had come to him, his secretary watching me. I tore this box open, knowing by its shape it wasn't books, and inside I found a brand-new, bright white, beautiful pair of running shoes.

Damn it.

I wanted to say something else, to say something stronger, but his sweet young secretary, fresh out of one convent and eventually headed for another, was there with me, kneeling beside me as soon as she heard me gasp, her arms tight around me.

Damn it.

So yes, that was bad. It was a weird coincidence, and not one of those good ones you hear about, the kind that give solace. But the moment those first few weeks that shocked me and grieved me more than almost anything, that was more about just grieving something that happened in the past and pointed me to the shape of the future, was the simple—what I thought would surely be mindless—task of filling out the boys' school registrations for the next year.

Just names on lines, just information. Their names, their ages, their grades next year. The next line was my name, my occupation, my work phone, my religion. Then, of course, his.

Father's name. Occupation. Work phone. Religion.

And . . . there was nothing to write there. He wasn't around, just living in another town or state. He wasn't deployed, as a military parent might be, gone, but due back. He wasn't even comatose in a hospital or quietly waiting for me to bring the boys to visit in a rehabilitation facility.

Deceased.

The wound felt sharp and deep, deeper still because I felt it as it dug, not only into my own heart, but as it must feel in two other hearts in particular, and it was one of those moments in which I couldn't help feeling afraid and even angry. My anger is never for my own sake; it's for theirs, two little fatherless boys, exploring the ruins.

⁓

A gorgeous day amid the broken things, this is. Katie lounges and thinks about whatever she is thinking. Reads a book. Poses for photos atop the pillars, positioning herself as if she's holding one of them up, as do the boys, who are still winning, still victors. I take a sweet photo of Michael giving Katie a kiss on the cheek as she perches on a large rock, ancient columns standing tall in the background. My mind, as it always is, is a riot of past and present.

I've got a couple of writing deadlines looming, and I wish I didn't have to work on them on my tiny netbook with my erratic Internet late at night on the farm in the middle of Sicily, but I really have no choice. That's what I do, and that's where the money for trips to Sicily comes from, after all.

There's something else on my mind, too. Something a little crazy. It's more than just on my mind, because what I'm doing is actually sitting here in Sicily seething about Michael Jackson. He apparently died a couple of days ago and what exactly did he think he was doing by pulling that stunt, dying at age fifty, of a heart attack? And what does the world think it's doing, mourning that lunatic? You know, of course, there was only one Michael, aged fifty, who died of a heart attack this year worth mourning. So yes, among all the other matters on my mind, I'm expending energy up here on the hill furious about Michael Jackson, Death Interloper.

But I am mostly thinking—because in a way it's always on my mind—about living life in the ruins. I wonder why we—I—find ancient ruins—even not so ancient ruins like collapsed barns and such—so attractive. Why do we wander about them, take photos, paint them? Why not just knock them down, pour fresh concrete, and build something new? Why preserve the ruins? How much of them do we keep and preserve at all costs? And how much do we just let crumble away into dust and disappear?

And now, as I do regularly, several times a day, perhaps, I pause and make an effort to correct myself. It's a coping mechanism, but it's also a spiritual discipline, and it's also very true.

For my life is actually *not* in ruins. Not at all. I, personally, am healthy; I have five healthy children who are all functional and seem generally content with life and are moving in positive directions, as we say. I'm not in any financial difficulties; I have a pretty easy way of making a living. Yes, yes, writing is challenging and draining, but it's not standing—yes, *standing*—at a grocery store checkout for eight hours; and it's not sitting in mind-numbing meaningless meetings; and it's not subsistence farming in a developing country.

My husband died. Husbands do that. Wives do that. Children die in their parents' arms. People are victimized and murdered, they are abused, they are consumed by cruel diseases of mind and body.

Michael took some steps on a treadmill and dropped to the ground, leaving us stunned but still here.

On vacation, for God's sake.

So yes, the metaphor of ruins strikes me as overwrought and I'm feeling abashed, once again, about my self-pity.

But then, I see them, the two little boys, huddled under a hunk of column tilted against another. It's me watching from a distance, them making plans and plotting more adventures in the ruins.

Just the two of them up there, climbing and descending, hiding and emerging to stand against the sun.

Maybe not so overwrought, after all.

~

I had seen a small sign for McDonald's as we approached Agrigento, and now, after we've finished with all the temples and catacombs we can manage for today, without telling them what I am up to, I direct the car up into the city on the hill to try to find it. They might enjoy a hamburger, and they will definitely enjoy some french fries after a week without that basic form of sustenance. Although if they'd selected pizza "American style" from any menu here, they would have found their french fries—as a pizza topping. Even I, who haven't really eaten anything from McDonald's in twenty years, might enjoy a french fry, honestly.

As the city thickens around the car, I finally confront what I've been dreading for weeks: those incredibly narrow winding roads up and down and around a steep hill, far more treacherous than Trapani, Monreale, or Palermo, crowded in by teetering buildings and markets, scooters zipping around me, more cars heading straight at me with only inches between the car's passenger side and stone walls that would surely take the car in any fight. Apart from the fact that I just can't find McDonald's, despite seeing a sign or two for it here or there, the driving turns out to be—well, not so bad, really.

It's not so bad . . . why? Because I'm a madly talented driver? Perhaps. Or perhaps because what eventually relaxes me behind the wheel is the sight of others accomplishing what I had sworn could not be done. Other human beings arc doing this thing. They're hugging those tight turns and squeezing past each other, they're veering close to the edge, they're managing. They get to where they're going. This can be done. And me? I can be one of the people doing it, too.

I never do find McDonald's, though. Agrigento is a small city, so I feel as if I have no excuse for that. But I do find that I can drive here. The ruins below me in the valley, navigating narrow roads in a lively little city on a hill, taking my cue from the confident: I find I can do it.

I don't buy fries back at Carrefour a few minutes later, but I do find some frozen chicken nuggets for the boys. Katie and I pick up the goods for what will be a spectacular supper, my ideal meal, the kind I could eat every day: bread, cured meats, cheeses. We find some blood orange juice and water. A two-euro bottle of wine. Katie heads back to the cheese counter by herself, and I watch her as she communicates with the cheesemonger, pointing out what she would like, nodding and answering a question. Laughing. We pick up some watermelon. The cart's loaded up, we're ready to go back to the farm for the evening, ready to eat, talk about the day, remember the ruins, and we're very ready to return to the dogs. We've got everything we need for now. Time to go.

This time, though, I pay with a credit card.

12

SUNDAY, MIDMORNING, MICHAEL RACES OUTDOORS TO join friends. He's barefoot, and I tell him he needs shoes.

"No, I don't," he retorts. "The lady in the green shirt who eats breakfast with us, she didn't wear shoes yesterday at breakfast."

If you threatened my life, I couldn't tell you what clothes anyone was wearing that morning or any morning on this trip, much less if they were wearing shoes.

As he's greeted by the dogs, who stand almost as tall as he does, I wonder what else he sees that I'm missing.

~

The lady in the green shirt (the American aunt) and her niece join us at the breakfast table although they have already eaten. The spread is much the same, the variation being the type of sweet bread—yesterday it was a sort of muffin, which was devoured; today it is a loaf with walnuts on top and apples within, which doesn't bring out the same level of enthusiasm from the boys.

We chat, and as always when fellow travelers talk, it is about what brought us here to this place. The aunt tells me more about their family history. I slip in, under my breath since Joseph is at the table, although distracted by the animals outside, that my husband died. I slip it in—driven, for that reason that eludes me, to tell. I want to raise the subject, but as usual, only with people I will never see again after this week.

Joseph, not hearing, not listening, takes two more bites and is off, out with the dogs.

~

I walk outside and stretch out in a lounger on the patio, waiting for Katie to wake up, waiting a few more minutes until it's time to dress for Mass. I love to watch the boys play with the dogs. It also breaks my heart.

For that's one of the things Mike always wanted, but we never could manage—a dog. He'd always had dogs growing up, and he talked about it a lot, about how great it would be to have a dog. I didn't object at all (well, not much)—even though my family never had a pet because of my mother's allergies—but it just never worked out for us. For nine years while we were living in Indiana, Mike kept saying that he was going to get a fence built around the backyard, and then we would get a dog, probably a Lab of some sort, but that never happened. When we moved to Alabama, he said that once we bought a house, we would be sure to get a dog. But that never happened, either. None of it did: the Alabama house together, the fence, or the dog.

So here we are in Sicily, just us, without him, Mike's boys falling in love with the dogs, and there's one more regret for you, but this morning, for once, the regrets don't hold me here. I pull away from them and keep moving, because I hear something. I watch boys and dogs running on the patio, hilly, pale yellow wheat fields behind them, cool pale blue morning sky spread overhead, and maybe it's my imagination, but something about right now hints at more beyond the regrets, a presence waiting beyond the absence. In the midst of panting, yelping dogs and gleeful boys, I hear what sounds something like a whisper of endless, joyful play once interrupted, but someday, never again.

~

Mass would start at ten, and we were ready to go by nine thirty, but Claudia and Marco didn't appear to lead us until almost ten minutes until the hour, so we arrive at the convent at some point in the middle of the second scripture reading. We've squeezed into an empty spot in a front pew of this chapel-in-the-round, and I'm listening to the youngish, but creeping-up-on middle age, portly and bearded priest preaching. I know that the Gospel today describes Jesus raising a little girl from the dead because for once I've prepared, having brought a booklet with the Mass readings for the month over from Alabama. I can sense the priest's passion as he preaches in a strong, sure voice, but all I can really understand is one word.

Morte.

Sometimes he says, *Fratelli e sorelle . . . brothers and sisters*, too, which makes my heart laugh and then crack a little because they're words Mike used to say a lot, just like that, affectionately imitating Pope Benedict, since that's a phrase that punctuated his homilies and other talks. So that's what I'm taking away right now:

Fratelli e sorelle. Morte.

The church isn't the dark little medieval chapel I'd expected and maybe even hoped for. It's bright and round, with high ceilings and abstract stained glass, and if this were 1972, I might say it's of a "contemporary" style. About a hundred of us sit in the pews and lean against the curved back wall. The nuns themselves, the Poor Clares—maybe twenty of them of various ages, certainly more younger sisters than you'd see in most American convents—are separated from us, of course, but not behind a screen as is usually the case in a cloistered monastery. Here, they're just sitting in chairs arranged behind the altar. Katie and Joseph are next to me, Michael's on the floor at my feet, and Claudia and Marco stand in the back, after having practically pushed us to this spot in the front row.

I sit here, crowded by my children, understanding nothing of the homily except that word *morte* and the general impression that the priest wants me to know that Jesus is victorious over death.

He'd better be. Really. Or else this is all a sham. I might as well get up and leave if what the priest is saying isn't true. This would be the case no matter what—why bother with it if you don't think it's true?—but especially now, with him talking to me about *morte*.

So do I believe it? If "hope" can be counted as "belief," probably, and if "confused" can also be counted, definitely. I work through all of that again sitting here, lurching between faith, doubt, certainty, and skepticism, trying to draw out presence from absence. The endless rumination that happens in grocery store lines, at stoplights, standing in my closet, or watching his sons run with dogs continues. I keep straining forward, pushing aside the curtains, which are so heavy and thick. Sometimes I can get a peek, but just when I do, those curtains fall back, just like that, everywhere, even here, while I'm sitting with the Poor Clares in Caltanissetta, listening to the priest say *morte* again and again.

~

The music here is not helping the cause, not pointing to heavenly choirs, because it is really surprisingly terrible. I had been hoping for some good basic chant, that steady movement of sound that seems to come from nowhere and moves on to eternity. Considering that these are cloistered nuns and all, it didn't seem unreasonable to expect that.

But this morning, there is not a hint of chant, and the dominant musical tone is that mournful, diffuse sound that all Italian congregations—in my limited exposure—seem to produce. I recognize one of the tunes as that of a song we used to sing in the 1970s, one written in a minor key, which doesn't help: "God and Man at Table Are Sat Down," which in the language-sensitive latter days of the twentieth century was renamed and grammatically disabled as "God and Us at Table Are Sat Down," the last time I heard it back home. I don't think they were singing anything about us or the table here in the convent, but the tune was there, familiar and in that sad minor key. We sounded like we could have been patients in a hospital recovery room.

I had also anticipated—correctly, this time—more or less mandatory Communion on the tongue because it's still the norm in Italy. What I couldn't have anticipated and didn't expect was the mode of distribution, which is a strange process in which you hold your own paten—the dish the server usually holds to catch a dropped host—in your own hand under your own chin, receiving, then turning and passing the plate to the person behind you in line. Joseph sees this process and, I can tell, quietly begins to freak out. He doesn't know what to do, he thinks he'll mess up. He's new to this anyway, for it's only been a few weeks since his own First Communion, back in May.

⤙

When I cleaned out Mike's desk at home, I discovered a stack of old black-and-white faded photos of him as a child. There's a little boy and his sisters goofing off in a backyard in New Hampshire forty years ago. A Cub Scout. A little boy proudly holding up a fish. That little boy with his dog. Another, the one I tack on my bulletin board above my desk, is of his First Communion. He stands in a blazer with some sort of badge on the lapel, hands folded at his chest, grinning. He's leaning a bit, as if he could barely be made to stand still for the picture, which wouldn't surprise me. He never did stand still for very long, anywhere, in my experience.

In the photo, Mike looks exactly like Joseph. That's not a wishful projection, either. It's startling how much they look alike. So much so that looking at that photo you would wonder why someone had antiqued this picture of Joseph and even tore up the edges a little for the full effect.

The morning of Joseph's First Communion, that May forty-three years after the boy in the picture's, as I got him dressed in his own suit and tucked in his shirt and brushed off his shoes, I saw that look on his face. Not the friendly grin that he shared with Mike in the photo, but something else.

The first few times it happened, in the weeks after Mike died, I scolded Joseph for that look, his lips twisted up in what looked like a smirk. I thought maybe he was hiding a forbidden snack in his mouth, so yes, I told him to stop it, to get that look off his face, right now.

But I learned the hard way—for him more than me—that he wasn't about to laugh and he wasn't eating anything. It's like his lips were screws that he must twist—hard—so that things would stay inside. When he looks like that, it turns out, the boy is just trying quite desperately not to cry. I didn't know that. If I'd taken just a minute those first few times and looked up from his mouth at his eyes, begging me, begging anyone—I would have known.

So that First Communion morning, as we finished dressing, for this big moment in growing up, in growing closer to God, I saw the look that seemed like a smirk but was nothing of the sort. I grabbed his hands in mine. His blue eyes filled with tears.

Daddy.

It's all he could say.

I know.

As usual, that's all I could answer.

Later that day, the day of Joseph's First Communion at Our Lady of Sorrows, a thunderstorm threatened, then struck before and during the Mass. Mike's sister remarked that this was entirely appropriate since Mike was always a big fan of the weather, which was true. If it wasn't sports, it was the Weather Channel on television when Mike had it on. Since he died I never know the forecast. I never have any idea what to expect when I step outside in the morning anymore.

The homily, given by the elderly pastor, concerned God's love. He did not tell us to prepare for death this time. No, today it was just *How much God loves us!* he exclaimed over and over. In another time, in another place, I might have tuned the priest out. It's a joke, you know, that in these modern times, all priests preach about is one more bland variation of *God is Love*. Thanks, Father Obvious. Been sitting here for forty years, hearing the same thing. Got it.

And so he went on that afternoon to all the little children, to all their families, reminding us. *God is love. Oh, see how much God loves us. He loves us so much he died for us, he gave himself to us, he gives himself to us here.*

He loves us . . . so much.

I kept half listening, kept trying to brush off the old news, but that time, sitting there with Joseph at my side and Mike dead, not sitting with us, I failed. That word kept pecking at my soul. *Love.* And then that other word. *God.*

I had to let the old priest's voice break through. If it's all so obvious, if I get it and can barely be bothered to listen, what's my problem? God loved—*loves*—Mike so much. He wouldn't create him just to have him disappear, to bring him into existence for a time just to have him not-exist. He still is. Somewhere, because God loved him and because he loved God back.

God loves Joseph, too—sitting beside me in his suit, uncomfortable, nervous, excited, and sad. God will provide for him—will fill the hole, will dry the tears. Somehow. Maybe even this way, right here. Or else, why are we bothering? Why have I dressed him up in his suit, and what do I hope he receives, as he stretches out his little hands for the first time?

After we receive Communion, I kneel next to Joseph and I sense just a hint of it. It wasn't a mystical ecstasy or a fearless certainty, but just that: a hint. For one moment in time—just a brief moment in that loving, dying, and now living Body, we were all there, together.

～

Back at the Poor Clares, we handle Communion without a hitch. Katie's in front of me, then I'm in front of Joseph, and after I receive, I simply turn and hold the paten under his chin for him, then pass it to the woman behind him myself.

Michael remains with Claudia, who's moved up to sit with him while we receive. He rests his hand on her leg, trusting.

I sit back after I receive Christ in Communion and I may have prayed for the Lamb of God to grant me peace before I went up there, but it's not happening yet, because, as usual, the battle continues: the battle to set the mourning aside and to focus on God Alone here, to not let Mike or his death reign as an idol in my soul. Because, you know, God is great, but I miss my husband a lot and I'm in agony for his boys.

So I try to call a truce. I try to shut up and stop arguing. I try to just let that Body live in mine. I do the only thing I can: wait.

～

After Mass we stand in the convent courtyard, and I pick up on what is clearly the ritual greeting of this day, what you are obliged to say:

Buona Domenica!

Happy Sunday is what they're saying. Good Sunday! For Sunday is, indeed, good. Sunday is about the One who lifted a little girl out of earthly death and then rose himself, breaking through the tomb, once and for all and even for us. Sunday is worth living for. Worth dying for. I myself should live for Sunday, I believe. A feast happens on Sunday; the saints gather in heaven and on earth. *Alleluia.* Sunday's good. Right? I hear the greetings echo, and I try to convince myself of the goodness of Sunday. That Sunday is true.

Claudia, Marco, and I stand there and talk about what we'll be doing for the day, *Buona Domenica* echoing around us. They are going to spend the afternoon with friends. I had spied a McDonald's on our way into town and I admit to them that we will go there for lunch—because honestly, on a Sunday at noon in a small, nontouristy city like Caltanissetta, there is not going to be much, if anything, else open anyway. And then, I say, we will head east to Piazza Armerina and take a look at the famous mosaics there in the ruins of the Roman Villa del Casale.

Claudia and Marco nod and approve of the choices (even McDonald's!). As he tells me the best way to get to Piazza Armerina, Marco stands next to Claudia, his hand casually resting on her shoulder, and right now I cannot take my eyes off them, off the simple gesture that speaks of friendship, trust, and just . . . love.

I'm jealous. Painfully jealous and struck hard by it standing there, watching them. Yes, I see couples all the time, all over the place. They're happy, entwined, chatting, embracing; they're young with a shared future, and they're old with a shared history, but none of them have affected me like this does right now: just Marco's hand on Claudia's shoulder, that's all, the two of them leaving Mass and moving on to the rest of their day, this good Sunday, together.

I used to have that. For just a little while, I had that, too, my best friend, my love with me, ready for another day—a very simple day—together. That day might have even been a Sunday. He might have just been watching football on the couch, then he would go out and toss a football or shoot baskets with the boys, and I would have been reading when he came back in and talked about getting a dog soon, and there we'd be. There we were. Now never, ever again.

How much do I hate this?

A lot.

Basically, I'm mad, furious at death.

Which is the way it should be, I think. Death should make me angry. It's not the way it's supposed to be, and if death isn't worth getting mad at, what was the point of that one Sunday morning two thousand years ago?

So yeah, I'm pissed off at death.

Screw you, death.

I suck it up, though, and I go ahead and tell Marco and Claudia, who are not death, and in fact are very nice people, that I hope they have a good Sunday, too. Then I walk quickly up the path from the convent to the cars, catching up to the children, who are far ahead trying to find the goats, and, oddly, a fawn, all of which Claudia had told them were kept by one of the sisters' neighbors.

Claudia and Marco continue to wish me a good day of travels, too, a good day of seeing new things. They call after me as they go to their car, the children and I to ours, they say it one more time:

Buona Domenica!

Good Sunday?

Well, like the kids say: *whatever.*

13

I T'S A McDONALD'S JUST LIKE ANY OTHER McDONALD'S, which, I suppose, is the whole point of a McDonald's. It's bright and clean and offers us burgers, chicken nuggets, and fries, but we do find some differences. The Happy Meal packaging is more elaborate—it's a boxy kind of divided tray. Happy Meals here also still included dessert (yogurt or fruit), which they haven't back home, I'm thinking, since Katie was small. Katie's salad is bigger, and, she says, tastes fresher. I pick at their fries, but don't get anything myself. Breakfast will keep me for a while. There's wine and beer on the menu, of course. Who would come if it wasn't?

A young family whom I recognize from Mass enters soon after we do. I see more customers nursing McFlurries than are downing hamburgers, and I say to them in my head, *You people can get real, authentic Italian gelato. What do you want with a McFlurry?*

But the main point of the McDonald's to me, right now? The bathrooms, of course. So far we have not run into any interesting bathroom adventures here in Sicily, and it isn't anything that worries me too much, not being too picky or of a delicate nature myself, but I'm still thinking it's going to be a good idea to hit this one before we move on—it's clean and a good place to change out of church clothes. After we figure out how to flush the toilet, that is.

(It's a button on the floor you push with your foot. Which again, like the cashiers with their stools, makes immediate, unimpeachable sense to me: so much more sanitary.)

McDonald's is also good for us because, in spite of those

minor differences of style, dessert, and beer, it is, indeed, familiar. The boys are ecstatic to be getting Happy Meal toys and eating french fries once again. We haven't been living in Mongolia the past few days, but it's not Alabama, either. Sometimes, as much as you're enjoying yourself, you want to touch base with the familiar. Sometimes it's all you need—just a momentary glimpse of what grounded you before. Then you can keep moving on to that new place, wherever it is.

So that's what we do. We leave the reassuring gleam of McDonald's and we head south to see something new to us: the famed mosaics at the ruins of the fourth-century Villa Romana del Casale, about forty kilometers southeast of where we are now.

Since there are hills and mountains in Sicily, there are also plenty of tunnels, and not long after leaving Caltanissetta, we plunge into one of them. Immediately, everything seems wrong to me. I cannot figure out what it is, but I'm so disoriented, I edge up as close to panic as I have in a while. In the next few more seconds of driving, with the boys making the appreciative sounds they tend to do while in the middle of something very exciting like a tunnel, I realize what the problem is: I can't see a damn thing. This is not the way it's supposed to be, I realize, not even in a highway tunnel. Why can't I see anything? Why is it so dark?

In another second, I grasp the problem: there are no lights in here. No lights illuminating the tunnel and I hadn't turned on my headlights. I was totally unprepared for the darkness, but there I was in the middle of it, anyway.

When someone dies, you tend to think a lot about signs, about warnings, and what might have prepared you if you were paying attention and what actually did prepare you without you even knowing it.

So when I think about all of that myself, I always come back to *God Alone*, of course, and Mike's fixation on it. He had been through enough in his own life, had his ideals bumped around enough to know the truth of it, and knew himself well enough to also know the truth of what St. Paul says: we know God's presence, wisdom, and strength most powerfully when we accept our own foolishness and weakness

I argued with him about it—not about any of us being weak fools, and not with the basic truth of *God Alone*, but more about what it means to live that out in the world, since we are not disembodied spirits, but human beings in relationships and community. That's how we know God, after all: through others. We discussed it, and I chafed, but really, I knew he was right, and after he died, his stubborn certainty on that score seeped into my soul. It would seep out again, regularly, and I would continue to argue with it—with him—never really come to a firm place where I can figure out how to say both *God Alone* and *I miss my husband* and, most important, seeing fatherless little boys as part of some bigger plan.

But still. For all the sadness I felt, for all that aching, I never did fall so deep that I would call the place I was despair. I was never even close. I might not have been able to make sense of much, but the world never felt closed in, pointless, or absolutely dark. I wasn't crazy about life on earth without Mike, and felt sure it was better with him alive, but I never thought it wasn't worth living without him. That, I knew, even in my saddest moments, would be stupid, and there also was that day, that day at the side of his coffin, when I saw him and lost my fear. It wasn't darkness there. I didn't know what it was, but it wasn't exactly darkness.

I think about that a lot. About the weird irony of how him in my life prepared me for him dying.

All of which, in the end, isn't even about him or even me. Accepting his death means accepting death, period. Seeing him redeemed by God means seeing all of us redeemed, too, if we can only say yes to it.

⌒

After just a few seconds, we burst out of the darkness into the afternoon sun, and, as she has been doing almost nonstop since Caltanissetta, Katie is still talking. And talking and talking, as is her wont, God bless her, and usually I enjoy it because she's a smart, funny, interesting person, but right now I don't care about a single word she's saying. I mean, *I really don't care*. In fact, I can imagine stopping the car at the side of the road right now and just walking off by myself into one of these wheat fields and leaving them behind, all of them talking. I don't want to be this alone with three children—soon to be two when she goes to college—my only conversation partners, my only companions in life, through the days, weeks, months, and years ahead.

Oh, how I love them, and yes *God Alone*, and the tunnel is behind me and is never where I live, but oh, how I do want him back.

⌒

That would be better: for him to be here. How could it not be? What wouldn't be better with him alive again?

Everything would be back to normal. I would be able to see things about God and laugh at Mike's jokes and listen to his stories. The boys would have their father back here on earth to take them out Saturday mornings for their haircuts, followed by their trip to Sam's Club for free food samples and a case of water. His parents would have their son, his sisters, their big brother, on the other end of the phone line, any time they felt like hearing his voice. How could that not be better—a thousand times better than him being dead? Is this even a question?

If I stand in the kitchen as I think this, the image of him walking through the door, right now, takes my breath away. What would it be like if I heard that voice saying hello to me and saw that hand tossing his lunch bag up on top of the refrigerator and heard that heavy sigh he'd breathe out before telling me about his day?

Standing there, I can't think of a bad thing about it. It would make everything—every single thing—all right.

Well, for us at least. The wife, the sons, the parents, the sisters, and the friends, sure. But when I force myself to follow it through to the end, I have to admit that we are not the only ones with a stake here, in this fantasy. After all, here I am praying for him to be in heaven, but I'm also determined that it would be better if he just came back, wrenched away from the Beatific Vision and then tossed back into this world, where he'd have to trudge back to the office on Monday, struggle against sin, be frustrated with limitations, suffer from some illness or another, watch his children suffer (because they will, because we all do), and then die all over again?

Really?

To wish that on someone? That's *love*?

⁓

After I turn on my headlights, after a few more tunnels and many more hills, after we park in the near-empty gravel lot, the first thing that happens at the Villa Romana del Casale is that when I speak to the parking lot attendant in Italian, he responds by asking if I am German. *Allemande?* Too much time listening to that German pope, he of *fratelli e sorelle* fame, speak Italian, I imagine.

The second thing that happens is a verbal altercation I witness between the girl taking tickets and an older man in line ahead of me. I think the point of contention is whether or not an audio guide to the site is included in the price. The two of them just go on and on, him energetically, she far more laconically, but just as determined. The man's wife stands behind him, clearly embarrassed until she can finally tug him away, headphones—or whatever the point was—denied.

I ask the girl if she speaks English. Yes, she does. I ask her what that was all about.

"Who knows?" She shrugs.

The last thing that happens to us at Villa Romana del Casale is that I must forcefully insert myself in between my daughter and a sixtyish postcard vendor who is picking out cards he says he wants us to have for free, but who is also repeatedly putting his arm around her waist as he makes his selections. She keeps edging away, but is trapped by a table and a postcard rack. So I get in there, push, and pull her away. That happens, too.

But before that last thing—which was really not scary, just weird and quickly halted—we studied tiny stones arranged on patterns on an ancient floor that I'd thought before I came might be interesting, but did not expect to remind me of death, but really, should I have been surprised?

~

Villa Romana del Casale is a little mysterious. The site is located in a valley about five kilometers from the hilltop town of Piazza Armerina. The villa complex, quite large, with many rooms, was probably constructed in the early fourth century. Like Pompeii, natural disaster (a landslide, it's thought) hid the original structures at some point until they were rediscovered and excavated in the twentieth century.

Scholars assume that the villa belonged to an aristocrat or perhaps even a member of the Roman Imperial family itself. Diocletian is mentioned. Whoever they were, they're dead now, and all that's really left of them and their house is the floor.

So, here we are, come to study that: their floor. The walkways for viewing are constructed about ten feet above, along the outlines of the former walls, and since they seem a lot like bridges, the boys find that awesome. Plastic sheeting is our ceiling now, which the boys also think is great because it seems like a big tent, but all I can think of is what a miserable hothouse this must be with lots of people crowding the walkways and the sun beating down.

Neither of those things are happening now, though. This may be one of the most popular tourist sites in Sicily, but today we're alone. I have no idea where the disgruntled man and his wife have gone; no one else shares these walkways with us, and the sun has disappeared behind clouds, so it is quiet and comfortable. Right now, this great villa and its spectacular floors belong to us, and we don't have to hurry, because we're not pressed by crowds behind us.

The boys are absolutely fascinated—well, Joseph is more so, for remember that Michael is only four years old and mostly likes to run around. But all his older brother needs is some leading questions to get him fully involved.

Can you find all the labors of Hercules?

How many animals are in this?

This one shows a lot of different ways of hunting. Let's find them.

And he's off. Counting, categorizing, making lists, taking out his little notebook and drawing.

They're absorbed in the bigness of it, as well as the details. They talk about how hard it would be to make such pictures out of tiny stones. I think about that too, as I think about the motivation for detailing the way you live in such a permanent way that will last so much longer than you will.

We can see it all, for every floor of the gathering spaces, the dining halls, the bedrooms, and the hallways tell us a story. We can see how they hunted, how they fought, how they traveled to Rome, how they dressed, and even how they played. One of the more well-known mosaics from the villa portrays some young women exercising, and because of the way they're dressed in brief, rather modern-looking separates, they're known as the "Bikini Girls."

The mosaics burst with animals—beasts being hunted down for food, fish and other sea creatures being taken from the sea by winged figures. The majestic Corridor of the Great Hunt, which I think I could stand and examine for hours, is my favorite. It boasts of the breadth and might of the empire, as elephants, rhinoceros, tigers, and lions are shown being trapped in African and Asian jungles and paraded back to Rome.

With the Triclinium, though, they are elevated to an entirely different level. It's an enormous, circular formal dining space. We walk into this room—well, actually above it on the walkways, of course, and we meet a hero. Hercules is here, hard at work on all his labors. This is convenient, because Joseph has been on a mythology kick of late, although he still tends to get the adventures of Hercules, Odysseus, and Perseus confused. Or maybe it's just me who does that and he actually has it all straight.

Hercules' muscles bulge all over his body, the stones artfully laid so that the shading alerts us to their size, how dangerous they could be in motion. We follow his labors around the room, watch him fight and spear and gain victory, and I imagine the courtiers, the flatterers, the rulers lounging, indulging in that moment, confident that this mighty Hercules reflects some truth about them.

And now, I think, not surprisingly, *they're all dead*.

There was a time in which walking above the mosaics would have sent me spinning downward, would have plunged me, if not into absolute darkness, into a very fearful place. Since Mike died that doesn't happen anymore. But I still can't help but think about how they're all dead.

I think about it in a different way now, though, for what settles in my soul as I contemplate all of us dead or dying is almost . . . satisfaction. It's one of the many odd and, to some perhaps, conflicting emotions that live in me now. I'm not happy that Mike died, but I'm more at home with death now. I don't like it, but I can look it in the face now, because, well, I have.

I find my mixed, conflicting, warring sensibilities echoed in the boys' reactions sometimes as well. For sometimes Joseph, especially, is struck by grief. He screws up those lips, he buries his head in my neck, whispering *Daddy*.

But then there is this thing that's happened a few times since Mike died that baffles me. The boys will be sitting in the backseat and I'll hear Joseph asking Michael a question under his breath.

"Where's Daddy?" he's asking.

Michael says nothing. I don't turn around, but I can almost feel him searching the back of my head, looking for a hint about what's okay to say.

Again, Joseph goads. Then again and again, "Where's Daddy?," he pesters until Michael practically explodes with it:

"Daddy's DEAD!" he shouts.

The oddness doesn't stop then, with the explosion. There are no tears or anger. There's just a bizarre, jokey, teasing vibe that's coming from back there, and I just can't decide what it's about, unless it's brothers trying to get each other into trouble, which is always a possibility, even now. Neither death nor life will ever come in the way of that, it seems.

But there it is, right there: a fact.

Daddy's dead. All the people who paid for these floors to commemorate their greatness are dead, all those who toiled under the hot sun laying the tiles are dead, and someday, sooner or later, all of us standing here looking at it will be dead, too.

I went to Mass not long after Mike died. The priest preached a homily about Jesus in the Garden of Gethsemane, that agony in the garden in which Jesus prayed that the cup he was about to drink be taken from him.

The priest pointed out that it wasn't. That Jesus drank from this cup, as would we all. He suffered. He died.

I sat there, stunned. Not because this was big news to me, but because I had never really confronted my own hubris about that cup. I realized that as much lip service I gave to accepting the truth of death, deep down, I didn't believe it would apply to me.

I've got this huge image of the dead Christ lain out on a slab at my left as I sit in Mass every week, and I am still convinced that the fact that my husband was lain out like that was a wild, weird aberration?

So as we climb up and down stairs and consider the gorgeous work of hands now less than dust in the air floating around us, mixed with the earth somewhere unknown, I feel, as I always do, perplexed at the mystery, but the one thing I don't feel now is afraid. I also don't feel alone anymore in that. For the priest held up Christ's cup to me that day, and since then there's been just this tiny, growing part in me that thinks of death not as solitary, frightful stillness, but as something that is not just mine, but ours. And for some reason, that brings me peace. I don't want to be alone. And in death, I know now, I'm not.

⌒

There was that day back in Birmingham that I went to lunch with some of Mike's coworkers in the diocese, including the bishop. It was that day, at the end of my first week of working at his job, that it hit me how foolish this was, this trying to keep him alive by taking his job.

Something else happened that day, too.

As we left the Magic City Grille that day, the bishop introduced me to one of the waitresses.

Do you remember the fellow who used to come here for lunch with me? he said to her. *The fellow with the beard? Well, he died a couple of weeks ago and this is his wife.*

He was holding up one of his Mass cards, one of those cards that said "God Alone," but she ignored him because she was busy with me. She grabbed me up in her arms—hard, and rocked back and forth with me and I was crying. He had been dead two weeks and I felt only half there.

Oh, honey! she said. *Don't you be sad! You know he's up there right now, havin' a party, dancin' a jig! He's happy! He's free from all this!*

She was right, of course. I know it, but still:

Lord, help my unbelief.

14

MONDAY MORNING, I'M SITTING IN MY IDLING, PUT-tering little car, somewhere in Delia, Sicily, wondering what to do next. The boys are in the backseat playing a video game until we get to someplace definite that I will force them to look at and be interested in. Katie's back at the farm. Even though it's summer, the girl still has an essay to work on, because she's an International Baccalaureate student, and summer is just another six-letter word to those people, apparently. Her ankle is also still smarting from a tumble down some stairs she took at the Villa Romana yesterday. After a week, too, I can tell she could use a break from us. A day by the pool, away from little brothers and (aimless) Tour Guide Mom, sounded just right.

So the boys and I came here to Delia. Why? It's not far from the farm—only about six kilometers—and is my requisite "proba-bly, maybe picturesque Sicilian hilltop town," this one known for a round, twisty pastry called *cuddrireddra*. That seemed enough reason for a quick morning trip.

But now we're here, and I have, in the few minutes I've navi-gated these town roads busy with Monday morning life, man-aged to lose even the vague interest I had in being here. I don't know what I thought this would be, but it's not it, and I can't find the *centro*—the central point of any Italian town, often with some sort of plaza, no matter how small, as well as a church or two. I don't see any of the usual signs pointing me to that cen-tro, no crosses rise above the roofs, cuddrireddra didn't really sound all that great, I think, and as I'm sitting at this intersection, I just can't determine a focus for this place, and I instantly lose mine.

The boys are too absorbed in their video game to ask what in the world I'm doing as I mutter something about getting pastries at Carrefour, then backtrack and head out of Delia. I end up leaving on a different road from the one I came in on, and I'm about to turn around, when I spy a small hill on the side a couple hundred meters ahead. On top of that hill, I can see a cross. So I keep driving that way, because I have to see what the cross on that small steep hill by the side of the road is all about.

I pull off the road, take out my camera, and leave the boys in the car as I climb the steep path up the hill. It's a shabby, worn spot lined with thistles; and I kick aside broken glass and trash as I go. Another reason to have left them in the car. The cross I'd seen stands atop a roadside shrine, shabby and gray, constructed out of poured concrete. It's shaped like a hut, with a peaked roof. The name carved across the top tells me whose shrine this is: *S. Giuseppe.* St. Joseph.

Someone has painted the initials "R.M." with a heart next to the locked grate in front, behind which stands a crucifix and a single glass candle holder on a small altar in front. Behind that altar I see St. Joseph holding the Child. They are clean and brightly painted and look far newer than the shrine itself. A small vase of sunflowers rises beside them. I wonder when this might be unlocked, when you are allowed to do more than drive by and see St. Joseph from a distance.

St. Joseph. Of course, after a directionless drive, I would end up at St. Joseph, for in a way, I think as I'm standing there, after a fairly directionless, reactive life, I ended up at the altar in St. Joseph's Church, marrying Mike. Who for his part had a deep devotion to St. Joseph—remember the oil—and who was praying in front of a statue of St. Joseph when it came into his head and heart, *Do not be afraid to take Amy as your wife.*

Because apparently, I'm that scary?

I don't know. Probably. But thanks, St. Joseph, anyway; thanks to you at your ramshackle little shrine I've found—or been led to—by accident, in the middle of a morning's wandering. For favors granted, for nine years, for two little boys, one named after you, thank you.

I pray and wish I had a candle to light, I take photos, and I pick my way through the trash back down the hill to my Joseph (and Michael) waiting in the car, wondering where I am going to take them next. That, I really can't say.

Back down and heading out west, a driveway curving away from the road down the hill catches my eye on the right. It leads, I can see, down to a collection of small buildings. They're of uniform size, but in different styles; they're connected, quite clean, and there are several rows of them lined up on what seem to be tiny streets. I really can't imagine what this place could be.

I've passed it as soon as I see it, so I pull one of those easy uncomplicated U-turns that makes me feel like I'm a regular Italian or something, and I swing back by and down the drive to see whatever this is. My exploration is stopped short by a closed gate and gatehouse. I study the structures as the car idles—they look like small houses, no bigger than a single room each, constructed in rows, some with peaked roofs, some flat, some with columns. I wonder what this could be—some sort of architectural model for a planned community? A surprisingly elaborate prison or mental institution, given the walls surrounding it?

It's quiet, I don't see a living soul, and I'm only taking this all in for a minute when it hits me. Of course there's not a living soul. It is, indeed, a city. It's a city of the dead. A necropolis.

The boys pause in their game, look through the car window, and ask where we are.

I say I really don't know, but what I do know is that there's supposed to be a castle somewhere around here. We'll look for the castle now, is what I say, as I make yet another U-turn and speed away.

I've read a lot of stupid theological speculation in my life, a lot of scholars and amateurs positing that the resurrection accounts were, if not outright mythological fabrications, maybe not literal truth either, and maybe what happened was that Jesus's friends were so overwhelmed by his continued spiritual presence among them, that it was so vivid, it was as if he were really there, and all they could do was dramatize that feeling in these stories about empty tombs and breakfast by the Sea of Galilee,

I never bought it, and even less so after my husband died, after I stood there for four hours at his open casket at the viewing. Standing there, I came to believe that anyone who thought that the witnesses to the resurrection were really just coping in a spectacularly imaginative way—well, those people have never been around a dead body, and for sure have never been around the dead body of someone they love and can't believe they've lost.

Because I'd know the difference between even the strongest intuition of a presence and the very real presence of the person I last saw lying in a casket if he walked in the door, tossed his lunchbox on top of the fridge, looked me in the eye, and said, *Well, hello there, sister.*

Those women who said they saw Jesus alive? Well, first, they saw Jesus dead. They did more than I did. They washed his cold heavy body, they wrapped it, and they were returning on that Sunday morning to those caves, that city of the dead outside the walls of Jerusalem to finish the work they had to stop because of the Sabbath.

Yeah, I'm pretty sure they would know the difference.

I know I would.

Delia's castle rises rather dramatically on a high mount south of the town. I don't have any trouble finding it. It's certainly majestic, but it's also in a state of collapse, jagged walls and crumbling towers pointing upward like a great sundial on this bright morning. It's also clearly inaccessible and closed up today. Signs indicate some kind of ongoing archaeological project, as well. Strike two, on the castle front. Since I operate out of a philosophy of minimizing children's expectations, the boys are not terribly disappointed, but they are, they both mention, castle already behind them, getting hungry. After all, they never did get that cuddrireddra.

Carrefour is only a few more kilometers down the road, so we go there to get food for lunch to take back to the farm. I drive in under the building as I did on Saturday and am surprised that the parking lot is so empty. In fact, it's totally empty. There's not another car in the place. We shouldn't even bother to get out of the car, but I do, not able to imagine that a mall would be closed on a Monday, but once again, I'm wrong. Not all day on Monday, but certainly closed now—it's 11:15, and the stores won't open until two.

This is starting to get on my nerves, these strange and unpredictable hours of Sicilian business. Of course, it's only unpredictable to me—everyone who lives here, who really needs to know, gets it and arranges their lives around it. Who am I to complain?

Pausing at intersections in my idling car and thinking things over is developing into the theme of the day. If I turn left here, I'll be back at the farm in fifteen minutes. It's still a little early for lunch, though. There's also no definitive reason to assume that Katie is even out of bed yet. If I turn right, the road sign tells me, I'll be in a place called Racalmuto. There's no traffic behind to pressure me to move on, so I whip open the map and quickly thumb through my *Blue Guide* to see what Racalmuto might be about. It gets more than a paragraph, I see—more than Delia did—so it might just be worth an hour of our time. If we can arrive before noon, before everything shuts down, maybe we can see something. One thing, at least. Who knows what that one thing will be, and I'm fine with whatever it is. Somewhere between aimless and purposeful, that's me.

～

Well, the center is easier to find in Racalmuto than it was in Delia, for there are signs—*Centro*—leading me right there, and even to a parking place off the vast, rectangular, and now very hot square. The usual plain-looking church borders the lot, and the door is open. Better hurry, I say, it's almost noon, we know what that means, and the little American boys are starting to figure it out, too, so they don't argue.

Walking in, we're startled as a life-sized statue of (of course) Padre Pio greets us—and I mean, practically greets us, his hand outstretched. He's almost striding toward us, and he looks quite real, quite alive.

Beside the usual image of the holy friar, we're greeted by something else as well: the surprise that I'm now growing to expect: an exuberant, riotous interior decor that contrasts so vividly with the plainness of the exterior. We move in closer and we seem to be surrounded by side and front altars as well as walls of marvelously colored marble—all pinks and greens and grays.

Except it's not.

I step up to one of the altars and look closely at it, study the surface, which does, indeed, to the eye, appear to be marble. I rap my knuckles against it and invite the boys to do the same. They look up at me in wonder.

"It's not marble! It's wood!"

Indeed—I've seen all kinds of trompe l'oeil before, but this really trumps them all. The boys walk around the church, rapping every side altar with their little knuckles, listening to what looks like solid stone ring out, hollow. I can't even imagine how this was done, and I'm simply amazed by the creativity and passion we encounter in a small church off a small square in a small town in Sicily.

⌒

One day in late May, a month ago, we were driving into the apartment complex, which was, like all the towns we're exploring here, set atop a hill. We were making our way up and were about to pass a figure on the right, a guy obviously on his way back from the pool, towel slung over his shoulder, small cooler in hand. We were all going in the same direction, us in the car, him walking, his back to us, up the hill.

Michael shouted from the backseat.

Daddy!

It's Daddy!

My own heart stopped, it seemed, stopped for him, for me, for all of us, but especially for Joseph. I couldn't see his face right away, so I could only wonder if just for a brief moment, his little soul had opened up in astonished joy at the possibility that his father had come back, had enjoyed an afternoon at the pool, and would meet us at home.

No, it's not, Michael, it can't . . .

YES, it was! It's Daddy! He came back to life!

He really said that. Michael said—*He came back to life!*

He was utterly convinced.

We passed the fellow so little Michael could turn around in his seat and see that no, Daddy had not, indeed, come back to life.

He wasn't crushed though, because that boy never is. He just settled back, a little abashed, but still smiling. As he did often those days, he posed a hypothetical question, using his usual contraction of his own making.

Wuff, he says—"what if"—*wuff it* was *Daddy?*

If it was, I'm thinking, we'd know it for sure. There would be no mistake.

There's a name for what that would be, I also think. I'm pretty sure that what they call that is *good news*.

I've been driven out of churches for the *reposa* many times—insistent wood clappers in St. Ignazio in Rome telling us to get out, as the bells chimed one, I remember in particular. Here, I realize only gradually that it must be time to close, for the front door has been locked. We're not being rushed, though—the side door is still open and there the watchman sits, cheerfully chatting with a female friend. They wave as we leave.

It is time for lunch, but a quick walk up and down the street in front of the church reveals no place in which I feel comfortable entering. There are little places scattered between the shops, but at the tables in front of all of them, men sit, nursing glasses, staring.

Yesterday after we had seen the mosaics, we made two stops, one in the town of Piazza Armerina, and the other in the smaller town of Pietraperzia, closer to the farm. We'd walked around the former, looked into its own gorgeous church, decorated in a very distinct blue and white that reminded me of Wedgewood pottery. We'd also attempted gelato up there, but as I paused at the door of one place, I was stopped short by what I experienced as an invisible wall, thrown up by the men sitting at tables between the door and the gelato, unsmiling men who looked up as I stood there, and just stared. They were there an hour later in Pietraperzia, too, tables of men outside the gelateria I'd seen, older men who stopped their conversations and looked at us skeptically as we moved past.

And it's the same here, in and outside of every place with tables, food, and drink. No women in sight, no children. Just us and the guys, here in Racalmuto. We'll grab a snack and then find sandwiches in an autogrill on the highway, I decide, without much trouble. I have no interest in breaking these barriers. Let them keep them up, if they want.

There's another fellow on the main street, standing quite still. He's wearing a suit, his hat is on his head, and he's holding a cigarette between his fingers. Except for his all-over bronze coloring, he looks almost alive, but Leonardo Sciascia, Racalmuto's most renowned citizen, has been dead for a while. Sciascia was a novelist, essayist, and social and political critic who held up the closed, protective nature of Sicilian culture to light. He was born here and spent much of his life here in Racalmuto, as well as in Caltanissetta up the road, where we'd been to Mass with the Poor Clares just yesterday. Michael is fascinated, can't get over the metal man in the street, and is especially taken with the cigarette.

Back in the car, I don't take an absolutely straight path to the highway that will take us back to the farm and this time, it's sort of on purpose. From a crossroads just outside town, I can see another road that leads northeast from Racalmuto, which winds up the edge of a hill. I would really like to drive on that road for a bit. Everything I've seen so far today has given me something interesting to think about. I wonder who goes to honor S. Giuseppe in his concrete shrine outside of Delia, why Sicilian cemeteries are built like little towns, who lived in the crumbling castle and who is studying it now and what are they finding out, what Sciascia had to say about Racalmuto, and it about him, how artists can make wood look like marble, and what it is I'm supposed to take away from Padre Pio showing up in every church I see.

All this, and it's only noon.

There's a clearing at a high point of this rising road. We can park for a minute and look back down into the valley, to Racalmuto. Here in the clearing, up so high, is, of course, a shrine. This one is a hut, too, the stony, peaked roof cracked in four places, but still holding. We peer inside the grate and see not a statue, but just a print of St. Anthony cradling Baby Jesus. Flowers stuck in a one-liter water bottle stand beside him, and on the small marble slab in front, a single candle burns, a flame flickering, a glowing column of bright red plastic with Padre Pio's picture pasted on front.

We can see a great distance from where we're standing, those little boys and I. They step carefully around the serious number of burned-out red plastic candle holders scattered in the dry grass at our feet around the shrine. Below me lie the places I've been today. I can't see them, but I know what's down there: statues that look like people, simple wood that looks like precious marble, and beyond it, beyond my sight at the moment, what looks like nothing I've ever seen before: the quiet stillness of the city of the dead. It's beyond my horizon right now, but I know it's there, because it always is.

Up here, always on a hill, it seems, the saints look out at me from behind bars. Their faces are faded and worn by the sun and wind, but their eyes are clear, and they always carry Christ in their arms.

Don't worry, they tell me. *You know that thing you think about all the time? Death?*

Don't be fooled.

It's not what it looks like, at all.

15

SICILY IS SHOWING ITSELF TO BE GREAT FOR MANY things, but right now, it seems to me that Sicily is particularly great for giving us intriguing little adventures in very short amounts of time. For as much as we have experienced so far today, Carrefour is still not open and won't be for half an hour. Since I don't want to wait that long, I stop for sandwiches at an autogrill. That's an Italian roadside convenience store, like a 7-Eleven, but with a fancier coffeepot.

Unbelievably, the guy behind the counter asks if I'm *Allemande*. As I wait for the food, the boys examine the gadgets and toys for sale, and the two fellows behind the counter silently watch me wait; that feeling of mild unease I've felt at times over the past couple of days returns, throwing a shadow on my occasional, but regular fantasies about actually (maybe, perhaps) moving here for a while. No, I'm not offended at being continually mistaken for a German person, but I'm feeling out of place since I sense the sight of me—a woman out on the road alone with children, as common as it is at home, is rare around here.

Believe me, I want to say, *it's a mystery to me, too.*

⌒

Back at the farm, Katie is lounging outside, talking to the American aunt and niece. She says she has read a bit and her ankle is feeling better. I wish she had seen the trompe l'oeil, Sciascia striding down the street in Racalmuto, and the saints on hills in their run-down shrines, but it's better in the end that she stayed here. She needed to work, she needed a break from us—*all* of us. She seems more than content.

The boys eat bites of the not-very-appetizing slimy ham sandwiches, then test out the water in the pool but judge it too cold for a swim. I study the map and decide that if we leave now, we can pull off a visit to the Macalube. I remind Joseph and Michael what the Macalube is, I tell them how long it will take to get there, and ask if they'd like to give it a shot. They remember the pictures I'd shown them on the Internet back home and they say yes, they want to go because those sound cool. They'd like to go check out the little volcanoes. They would.

❧

The most frequent question I'm asked since Mike died is, naturally, "How are the children doing?" (And after that—*What are you going to do now?*) It's an understandable question, and a good one.

The counselor tells me to watch their behavior for what we all know is called "acting out," and so far, aside from Joseph's mysterious goadings of Michael into yelling, "Daddy's dead!," life seems normal and healthy, but I still can't help but be convinced that this cannot possibly end well. That at some point, this year, the next, thirty years down the line, it will all come to the surface, it will all explode and when it does, it will all be my fault. Even though it was his heart that killed Mike, not me, it will somehow, still, all be my fault.

It's everything: the general situation of little boys losing a father, the specifics of them losing *this* father, my own fatigue, my age, my own weakness, confronted with this task of trying to compensate for the loss, which is what I think I need to do.

On the Saturday after that first Fun Friday, the boys decided they'd like to see a movie. Now, this had been Mike's job, and he embraced it willingly, not because he enjoyed stupid kids' movies, but because he liked sitting there and eating movie popcorn.

Whatever they wanted to see, he was game, which was a huge relief to me, because after all these years, my tolerance for kid movies has definitely reached its limit.

But they wanted to go on the first Saturday after the first Fun Friday, so we did. They chose *Bolt*, which was by then showing at the dollar theater. It's an animated feature about a dog who thinks he's really the superhero dog he plays on television. It was the usual experience of those days: I was depressed, the heartfelt song in the last part of the movie about home made me even more depressed, they were mostly excited and happy with perhaps a moment or two in the midst of it in which they paused, looked around, and, as they considered who was missing and what was different, pressed up against me, arms around my neck and I just said *I know.*

It was like this a lot, doing the things Mike did with them: taking them for haircuts Saturday morning, taking them out for breakfast before the haircuts—I'm not a breakfast eater, especially of the carb and grease-heavy American kind of breakfast—but they all loved breakfast, so we went out on another Saturday morning, and all I could see were fathers and sons in baseball uniforms gathered in the restaurant, obviously on their way to some tournament. Just lots and lots of fathers and sons as far as I could see.

I could not, as I said, imagine that this would end well, even though I believed that Mike was still their father and would intercede for them and pray for them and now, in intimacy with God, could actually do more for them than he could when he was on earth. I prayed.

So, I worry, but I also know. I know what life has taught me after all these many, many years (!) and what I've told my older children, deep in their own struggles and feelings of different kinds of loss and different missing pieces: this, what you feel, is everyone's lot. No matter how they present themselves, no matter how confident they seem, everyone is walking around with a hole, a resentment, a question, a nagging sense that something is not right, the suspicion that if this or that aspect of their life had been different, they would be happier, they would be at peace, they would be complete. *Be kind*, someone once said, *because everyone you meet is fighting a great battle.*

I know it's true, because that's me in the mirror.

And you just have to figure out that the only way out is God. Not a platitude, and not easy, either. You can resent your parents or your childhood classmates or your own limitations or poor choices or the person who went away day after day, year after year, and you can sit and dwell in them, wallow and blame. But they're all just there, most of them are in the past, arc things you don't have any control over anymore, if you ever did.

God Alone.

For God knows, God suffers, and there's that bridge again. When I think of Jesus, he's a bridge—that bridge between life and death, but he's that bridge, too, between the often quite wretched nature of life on earth with all its ways of failure, betrayal, and misdirection, and life where we're whole.

Jesus have mercy on me a sinner. It's the Eastern Christian Jesus prayer that you repeat over and over—like a mantra, but far better because it's not about reaching nothing but rather finding your way out of nothing, and not even to something but to Someone. Someone who suffered too, someone who died, too.

All I want to do is to be able to help these boys be there. To recognize the weakness, the hole, and admit what's bubbling there and to let it flow to Mercy.

Help me is my main prayer these days, and some days, it's all I've got.

~

The way to the little volcanoes takes us past the Carrefour yet one more time today, and then to a turn west a few kilometers before Agrigento. We drive through the outskirts of a town called

Aragona, through a depressing stretch of half-constructed apartment buildings where work seems to have been abandoned a good while ago. At a crossroads, I see a wooden sign that, just by its rustic appearance, seems to point me to something involving nature. So we turn that way, we drive a little while, and now there seem to be these sheep.

They come at us over the crest of a hill, right in the middle of the road, dozens of sheep and goats in a hardy, healthy flock flowing around our car and the one ahead of us. The goats are mostly white with black heads and long black floppy ears, and the sheep are beautifully clean, white and recently shorn. Bells clanging, they pass, undistracted by the cars they've brought to a halt, led by dogs, followed by a man on a scooter.

The boys are naturally delighted. They reach out the windows and try to touch the animals. Even if I can't find any more signs or understand those I do, even if we don't manage to find the little volcanoes, the encounter with sheep and goats will certainly be something to remember. Our plans for the afternoon might fall through—you never know, there's always that possibility, since it happens at least once a day here—but the trip won't be wasted. We did, after all, see sheep.

～

Not long after we pass the sheep, I actually find the preserve. Parking—*Parcheggio*—is marked in a semicircle of dirt carved off the road. There's one other car there and a white dog sleeping next to it.

Men and boys work in the rippling pale yellow fields across the road, feeding wheat into machines.

I park and lock the car, stuffing everything of value with me into my backpack. I have no idea how long a hike is ahead of us or if my car will still be in sight when we arrive at the little volcanoes. I'm not taking any chances.

We walk in one direction for about a quarter of a mile, but

see only scrubby fields of grass and dirt and an empty house. We walk back around, try the other path, and of course, this—the path my instincts told me to take at first, which I ignored—is the right one. We reach a wooden shelter, some signs in Italian explaining what this is and what the rules of engagement are—and up over a little rise—*vulcanelli*.

At first, it looks like absolutely nothing. It looks like not a thing more than a big patch of gray, dusty earth, and I congratulate myself on my mad tourism skills, bringing us here to a patch of bare dirt. But then we step closer, squint, and study it. We let the landscape sink in, let ourselves be a part of it.

"It looks like the moon!" the boys cry, and they're absolutely right. It's like a lunar landscape here, dotted with craters and mounds. They race around madly at first, as they always do, but then they're stopped short by a bubble on the ground, a bubble that grows out of that gray earth for a few seconds until it pops and a most gentle flow of muddy gray oozes out of the hole. When they stop running and stay quiet, they can even hear the popping. They can hear tiny explosions all around them in the still, hot afternoon.

They are absolutely fascinated. They race from crater to crater, from mound to mound, tracking the little explosions, finding bigger ones every time, discovering new holes just beginning to break open. They balance on the rocks, they run in circles, they crouch down and wait and listen while what's underneath their feet transforms, takes shape, loses it, and, when the pressure's just right, bursts out.

~

We have been there for thirty minutes and the boys show no sign of wanting to leave, when my up-to-then unconcerned, take-it-as-it-comes vagabond mom freezes inside.

The car.

It's out of sight, a third of a mile away. Yes, I have everything with me, including a cell phone, but who knows if the cell phone will work out here and we truly are almost in the middle of nowhere, us and the little volcanoes and the wheat and the passing sheep.

What in the hell am I doing?

Tourists have been known to be hurt, to be kidnapped, to be killed. It's happened in Italy, in Sicily . . . anywhere.

This is all very adventurous, true; the place is different and fascinating and the boys love it, but I am possessed at that moment, uncharacteristically, by fear. I wonder if I have become just a little too cavalier. I have gone from imagining—not the Mafia, I never imagined the Mafia—but I did imagine carjackings and kidnappings before I came. I've gone from that, implied in the first page of my travel bible, to standing in this isolated spot with my little boys—Mike's little boys, left to me in trust to keep safe—the car out of my sight, even the sheep and their shepherd long past. I'm seized by the determination that we must get back to the car, now.

So without rushing, without letting on, just as I tried to not let on when I was lost looking for the salt, I begin to hustle them back. Hoping that all is well, that we can get out of here safely and get back to the farm, to their sister waiting by the pool, to dinner, to the dogs. I suspect, fear that all might not be well; I want to escort them safely through reality, but I don't want to frighten them, either, in case everything is really going to be all right after all.

Which it is. The other car is gone, but the dog's still there, dozing in the shade, under our little white car.

~

In the early evening, as the sun moves lower over the hills surrounding the farm, as the colors in the sky change from blues into pastels and purples, Katie and Joseph swim in the pool, Michael pursues and is pursued by a dog.

Katie carefully lifts a stranded, soggy bee out of the water and studies it off and on for a long time as it lies on the side struggling to dry off.

Marco comes home and we wish each other *Buona Sera*. He explains the pool—that this is a saltwater pool and he only puts chlorine in once a month. It's very interesting.

Michael keeps running back and forth from our apartment. He goes inside with a clean face, but upon every return, he has a mouth perfectly circled in chocolate. He wipes his face with a towel, races back in, returns minutes later, again with his chocolate mouth, laughing. He seems to believe that he's pulling something over on me.

Katie pulls Joseph around in the pool on a Styrofoam noodle, affecting a tour guide voice as they go. They can't stop laughing.

It's a beautiful evening. Dogs chasing boys, boys chasing dogs, girl swimming, observing, reading, new friends dropping by to chat.

I could say that it is fantastic and wonderful, and yes, I could say that if it were not for you in your casket. But you will always be in your casket, you will never come back to sit next to me at the pool, never play with the brothers, never tease and challenge Katie, no more eyes, wide and curious and ready to seek the absurd and the beautiful and then talk to me about it. The eyes are closed. The mouth is closed. Sewn shut, I've heard.

The sun is setting, pinks and oranges blanketing us from the west, flocks of birds are coursing over us like rivers. Life keeps flowing around me; today it courses on land and through the sky.

It's so beautiful. It is. It's so beautiful, I might just explode.

16

GRIEF, THEY SAY, *IS NOT A STRAIGHT LINE.*

No kidding, I say. Life isn't either, so what fool would expect grief to be any different?

A couple of times a week, my chauffeuring route takes me near the hospital. If I'm not paying attention, I end up sitting at an intersection with the huge red-and-white emergency room sign in my sights. On those same days and even on other days, I have to drive in the vicinity of the YMCA, and it seems to me that every time I am near either one, an ambulance is around too. It's sad and still kind of unbelievable, as in I sit in my car, study the door into the hospital, and think, *Really? Did that happen? Was Mike in there, dead?*

But then later at home, the memory of the hospital, the Y, and my helplessness still lingering in my heart, one of the boys will hug me, which of course means that the other will follow. It's simple, but quite powerful enough to wipe the image of the hospital from my memory. Little arms wrapped around me and soft young cheeks pressed against mine instantly turn me in another direction. I feel grace, purpose, and even gratitude.

I turn back, move forward, lurch backward, returning right back to where I started, my sad self rounding a sharp turn and meeting my almost-peaceful self right at the bend. I smile a little, I cry a lot, and I rebuke myself constantly for my shortsightedness, selfishness, and lack of faith. After all, he's in *heaven* (I'm praying), with *God*. Have a little faith, girl. Just a little, okay? And please stop being so selfish.

Haven't we been here before?

It starts to get old. I understand that *grief is not a straight line*, but I do wonder if I will ever arrive at a strong place made of rock, a place aboveground made of trust and faith. I also wonder if I have more control over the shape of the road than I let on. I wonder, as the weeks and months wear on, if I can do more to help myself. I wonder if I really had to drive by the hospital today at all, or if there isn't, in fact, another way to get where I'm going.

～

We've been twisting and turning for a while now on this Tuesday morning, riding through the Sicilian countryside west of Caltanissetta. As the crow flies, we are about forty kilometers northwest from the farm, but crows, as they fly, don't have to drive cars on roads that don't simply wind, but continually twist and turn in on themselves back and forth, over and over like so many pieces of Christmas ribbon candy laid out between here and there. So while we left at a fairly reasonable 9:45 this Tuesday morning, it's now about 11:30. It's taken us almost two hours to cover less than thirty miles. We are obviously not crows.

We're almost at the end of this road, though, because we see it, and as I look at what's ahead, I think that this is one of the most improbable things I've ever seen. Fields and hills surround this slightly rolling plain we're driving through and jutting up in the middle of it is a sudden, inexplicable hill of jagged stone, a sharp rise that looks as if it might have been thrust up from below by a giant's thumb.

And on top of the rudely intrusive rock, I finally discern our destination, which is, indeed, at last, a castle. It's not easy to pick out at first since it looks as if it might have been simply carved out of the rock itself. But it wasn't. Fresh stone was hauled up here six hundred years ago, piled high and shaped into broad strong walls by men with only carts and axes and carving tools, no electricity or engines, only animal energy to help them do it.

I see it, Katie sees it, the boys see it, and we're glad to see it, this castle of Chiaramonte, near the town of Mussomeli, but even the boys moderate their enthusiasm because there is that one point of uncertainty that dogs us everywhere in Sicily. That's certainly a castle up there. It's huge, solid, and not even crumbling. It might be the castle of our dreams, for some of us probably do indeed dream about castles.

But there's always that question: Will they let us in?

~

We see some sights on the morning's journey to the castle. We see ruined farmhouses, ancient conical-shaped huts that served as protection for herders and farmhands. And of course, we see many, many shrines. I drive past the smaller shrines, although I'm sure they have their stories and are worth a look, but this drive is taking us long enough as it is. But when I spy a roadside shrine that's larger, that's set up higher on a hill or that has a distinct design, I slow down, turn around if I've gone past it, and the kids hear me say yet one more time, "Okay, just this one—it will only take a minute."

This is what I say as I pull into a parking area on the side of the road about an hour after we get started. Katie mildly objects to me getting out for this one, not just because she wants to keep moving, but also because the place has a vaguely official air to it: the shrine on the small hill in front of us is accessible, but it's also close to a high wall constructed between the parking lot and something else. She thinks I'll be crossing a boundary of some sort, going where I'm not allowed.

A couple of men are yanking weeds, trimming and raking the small space in front of the shrine. I ask them, the best I can, if it's okay for me to walk up there. I point to myself, I wave my camera around, I point up to the shrine, I say, "Okay?" They open their arms and nod, welcoming me, almost as if they would love me to go up there and pay her a visit.

For this one belongs to Mary. The structure is much larger than St. Joseph's and St. Anthony's from yesterday, and it seems a bit newer, too. It's circular, topped by a peaked roof that seems to me to almost purposefully evoke the shape of those old herdsmen's huts in the fields.

Inside—and I can step inside because this shrine is larger than the others—I am surprised by an exquisite mosaic of the Madonna and Child, framed by two, not-exquisite, contemporary colored glass windows. But even the windows with their boring, formless design can't take away from the richness of the detail of this mother and child, the two of them holding a single rose together, the child with his other hand pointing to his small, but unmistakable Sacred Heart.

A few minutes later, a little farther down the road, I'm stopped short by what looks like a telephone booth on a loop in the road on a village's edge. This booth stands in the midst of some living plants and simple landscaping with a couple of bright green benches facing each other, all behind a low fence. Mary's here, too, not in mosaic or painted form, but life-sized, waiting in the booth behind locked glass doors. She's wearing a toga of sorts, so she looks more like an early Christian martyr, but the crown gives her true identity away.

Wouldn't it be great, I think as I drive away, to live in a place where every village, every neighborhood, and maybe every other street or so has a spot set aside where you can lay a flower, light a candle, and say a prayer for protection or gratitude? How different that would be, I think, to be regularly face-to-face with the invitation to offer it up—to offer candles, flowers, prayers lengthy and quick, complicated or in passing while you're rushing from one place to another—to offer up whatever ails you, whatever brings you joy, to lay it there, remembering, in hope, in despair, in gratitude.

If the castle is, indeed open now, around 11:40, I fully expect that this will be a brief tour, since the castle will also certainly close up at noon, not to reopen until four, like every other business, church, and shop on the island of Sicily. But for some reason, we discover when we get to the ticket window attended by two younger, clearly bored women, the castle is different. The reposa here doesn't begin until one.

That's a relief. We'll have time, and we'll have a lot of space, too, for ours is the only car in the parking lot. We're alone, just as we had practically been alone as we studied the mosaics at Villa Romana del Casale.

It's a broad path that leads up the rock to the fortress. It winds between scattered stones, both tiny and massive, and it's edged by thistles and wildflowers of pink, purple, and white. The path is not a short one and it's not easy, and as we move higher and higher, getting hotter and hotter, I crack open my teacher persona, inviting my sweaty group to imagine what it was like when people actually lived here, when they labored in their weighty clothes and carried their burdens on their backs or pulled clattering wooden carts right here, where we're walking now.

The castle was built in the late fourteenth century by Manfred Chiaramonte III, who lived here himself, followed in the next couple of centuries by his descendants and various other noblemen. Eventually, though, the castle dwellers abandoned the series of strong, notched walls that rise above the natural rock for good and moved into a more accessible villa nearby in the early seventeenth century. It was, for a time, used as a prison.

Speaking of prisons, for his part, my son Michael is totally about the castle dungeon. In the car, on the path, and now at the castle gate, he's obsessing, and he wants to know where it is. He must know where he can "THROW prisoners in the dungeon." Michael the dungeon keeper never just sends or escorts the condemned to the dungeon. The prisoners must be THROWN. He covets that job. He'll fight you for that job. He says "dungeon" six dozen times in the hour we spend at the castle.

At the gate, we consider the large stable area, now glassed in and pristine. We wander the beautifully restored rooms of the castle. A very few furnishings have been set up in them. There's a long table in the banquet room, an empty suit of armor in the corner. There's a prie-dieu (a small kneeler) in one corner of a bedroom, and of course, the hole in the ground in the lavatory is a big hit. I read aloud the Legend of the Three Women from the guidebook: the story being that one of the barons who lived here closed his three sisters up in a room above the ceiling for their own protection when a war broke out, leaving them with, he thought, enough provisions to last until his return. The war, unfortunately, went longer than anticipated, as sometimes happens with wars; the provisions ran out, and a castle haunting is born.

The walls are immovable, massive stone; the floors are solid under our feet; the ceilings are secure. Life used to live here, but it's empty now, unless you count the three sisters. The power that called all this into being is gone, and all that remains are stone rooms where little boys can run, tease empty suits of armor, and sit at head tables with mocking, serious faces, pretending they are the powers that were. They're certain that it would be awesome to live here back then when it was filled with life; they think that living today in their own world is surely not as interesting as it would be to live here, in the castle's past.

We've wandered in and out of bedrooms, banquet halls, and living areas, and we've circled around a few times, without seeing another soul. But this time, after yet another greeting of the silent knight in the corner, we see one. She wasn't there before, but now she is, sitting on the ledge of an arched window that's open to the valley spread out below.

She's talking on a cell phone, which she snaps shut once she sees us. *Ciao*, she says, then stands up and wordlessly points to a closed door. We'd attempted to open that door a minute ago—when she wasn't there—but found it to be locked. We obediently gather at the door, wait for her to unlock it, then follow her down narrow stone steps into another series of rooms—darker, of course, but much like the upper rooms in that they're clean and bear no indication of their use. Dungeons? Why not. Yes, these will be the dungeons.

The woman, in her midthirties, with her glasses, pink shirt, and chopped bleached hair, strides briskly ahead of us, saying nothing, not looking at us, not pausing once. I don't know Italian for "dungeon" or "prison," so I really can't ask, and besides, she's walking so fast, I'd have to run up and stop her in her tracks to do so. We glance at one another, totally at a loss. We don't know if we are supposed to stay and wander and she would be at the other door waiting, or if we are just supposed to follow her as she strides through the . . . apparent dungeon. We choose the latter course, just to be safe, so as not to be closed up in the dungeon ourselves, and at the end of our two-minute journey below, we tell her *grazie* as she locks the door behind us again at the first level. It was odd. But at least we saw that dungeon. Maybe.

~

Dungeons are, of course, dark. There's no apparent exit, no way out, and who can help falling into despair down there?

Sometimes I go online and read through discussion boards for the widows and widowers. Especially in those first few months I did, doing particular searches for keywords like "sudden" and "heart attack." Does everyone else, I wondered, find this not only sad but so very strange?

One of the things that struck me as I read through postings was the number of people who would write about their utter despair, of barely being able to get out of bed even a year after their husband or wife had died. How they couldn't see a way out.

I read those heartbreaking posts and I wondered why I've not been to that place. Part of it was his faith, his preaching *God Alone* at me for so long. But I am also pretty convinced there's another reason. I'm thinking it's prayer, and maybe not just my own.

After Mike died, so many people prayed for him and for us that it was almost embarrassing. Every day in those first few weeks, it seemed, I received news—a card, an e-mail, a note—of someone offering something up for Michael's soul and for our family.

Priests offered masses. Those going to Mass offered their participation and prayer at Mass, offered the Communion they received. There were rosaries and Holy Hours offered. He died right before Lent began, and two people wrote me to tell me that they offered their Lenten disciplines for that whole season for his soul and our peace.

The Monday night I got back from burying him in Florida, I ran through my voice mail. One was left in a woman's voice, a voice that was breathless, exhausted, but still trembling with energy. I had to listen to it three times to understand who it was and what she was saying.

She was an acquaintance. I didn't know her well, but I knew she was devout and she also had spent time with Mike on a Communion and Liberation retreat weekend in the early fall. She'd given birth that past Friday and had endured six hours of unmedicated labor before her daughter was born. Her voice mail told me that she had offered all of this, all her pain and struggle during those hours, offered it up for Mike's soul and for us.

She prayed, all those people prayed. I prayed too, of course. We were all praying. I also think about prayer a lot. I suspect that the thinking about the praying does not help the actual praying much, though. I often have to intentionally turn off that torrent of questions about how prayer works, and just crawl back to the Gospels. I think of Jesus, who tells me to pray and who also tells me how to pray. He should know. I listen to his mother, who then says, *Do whatever he tells you*, so yes I will. I'll try.

I think of C. S. Lewis, who answered the question his nephew wrote to him about prayer by saying certainly God could do anything. He could make the world work any way he pleased, and do it directly, without human help. But he didn't make it work that way. He involved us, and so we're a part of the way the world works, not only through our physical activity, but also through our prayer. Mysteriously, yes.

Who knows how it all works together or why. I certainly don't. All I know is that in those months after Michael died, I was kept out of the dungeon. Darkness waited beyond the door, but strangers stood in front of that door, praying. I'd turn and I'd twist on the road, I'd reach the bend where I couldn't see ahead or behind me, and I'd think I hadn't traveled any distance at all, but then I would see it: a candle lit by a friend or a stranger, left burning at the bend of yet another hairpin turn.

17

T HE YOUNG WOMAN BEHIND THE COUNTER AT LA CASA del Pane wears crisp white chef garb and an impressively tall toque on her head, which seems a little much for a tiny bakery on a side street in the small hill town of Mussomeli, Sicily.

Whatever the case—whether the formality is the norm or she is simply very proud to be a baker, what matters this early afternoon is that the young baker in the towering white hat is very kind to us. I buy ribbon cookies and the fig-filled pastries that Joseph has declared, since arriving in Sicily, to be his very favorites. The baker hands the boys some extra cookies and waves off my look, making clear they are a gift. With our bag of sweets, we head for the park around the corner, at the edge of the mountain looking down in the valley and over at the castle.

We'll sit here, the boys will play, we'll eat before deciding what we would like to happen next. As if we could even do that, right?

⌒

What was requested was a Pokémon cake. Or Star Wars, if Pokémon was unavailable.

So the Wednesday before Joseph's eighth birthday, two months after his father died, I started the journey to find a cake, which I assumed would be an easy one. The birthday party would be Friday, so this struck me as plenty of time.

Not so easy, though. The first grocery store bakery where we stopped had neither theme in its big, cartoon-stuffed cake decor book. Nor did the second or third. Of course you are thinking . . . *Why didn't she just make a cake and put Pokémon gear on top of it?* Because I wasn't thinking, that's why. I was mainly wondering how "celebrate" and "Mike's dead now" fit together, so no, I wasn't thinking.

We finally hit the Target near our apartment. Yes, *that* Target. And blessed be the day: Pokémon cakes! And not just one, but a choice of four designs in the cake design book! Joseph picked one, and we put in the order with the young guy on duty in the bakery that day; we joked about how we should have come there first since it was closest to our apartment anyway.

Phew. We were so relieved. Joseph was so excited.

Soon enough, it was Friday, about one in the afternoon. Michael and I drove the short distance to Target to pick up the cake. Joseph was still in school, to be fetched at three and then whisked down to the horror house with the animatronic rat and many very loud games for the party at four o'clock.

I presented the copy of my order slip to the woman behind the counter.

She glanced around the counter blankly, unconcerned.

"We don't have this order," she said. "I don't even see a copy here." She looked up at me. "And that's an old book anyway. We don't have Pokémon sets. Whoever took the order should have checked."

Indeed he should have. I kept my cool as she offered some other anime character instead but I decided—and told her—that after this they didn't deserve my business, so we rushed out, me trying to think how to fix this in the course of ninety minutes.

On the phone in the car I called the grocery store that lay in between Joseph's school and the robot rat house and was transferred to the bakery. I explained the situation to the lady on the other end, trying to hold back tears, trying not to let the subtext of the moment burst through. I said practical, earthly things about bright yellow and blue Japanese creatures and that an hour would be perfect, but I was really thinking something else:

You see, this is my son's eighth birthday, and his first one without his daddy, who died two months ago today—oh, in fact, it was at this very moment, about two in the afternoon, yes, two months ago today, I was sitting in the emergency room at the hospital, contemplating his broken heart and mine, and ours . . . please help me figure this out. If not all of it, just this one little thing. This cake.

The woman explained what the Target woman had said: that the Pokémon cake sets were old now, and no one had them anymore. But, she added, if I could bring in a picture of a Pokémon, she could put it through their scanner, which would produce an edible decoration for the cake. It was around 1:45 now, she was going to get off work at 2:00, but she would stay and get this done.

I didn't have time to go home and get a really good Pokémon picture—all I had in the car was the Pokémon card set I had just purchased at Target for a gift for him, so I tore it open and pulled out one of the card packs and hoped it would do.

She was just finishing up a cake when we arrived. We talked about the cake, she said she could enlarge the picture on the card. I took out a bill from my purse, knowing it was probably against the rules, but wanting to do something—"Can I give you—" I started. She waved it off. "It's all part of the job."

Of course I wanted to tell her—since I thought it was doubtful I'd ever see her again—I wanted to tell her about everything I was carrying in my heart, how heavy this was, and how she'd lightened that load, but I decided against it. Why should I burden her?

And, come to think of it, who knows what the guy at Target might have been carrying that made him forget what he was supposed do that day?

When Mike died, my relationship to the rest of the human

race shifted—not in one direction, but in a back-and-forth kind of way. I may feel different from almost everyone else I know, for I hardly know anyone my age whose spouse has died, but I also feel more in common with everyone I see because under every snappish reply, behind every forgetful sigh, I sense little volcanoes bubbling, I see invisible burdens everywhere, and I try to understand as I hope to be understood myself.

As for Joseph, he was very happy with the cake. He was so excited about the party—his first "real" birthday party—that he ended up not caring that this cake didn't come with plastic doodads, but just plain old frosting and a picture from a Pokémon pack. And he loved his party, loved his gifts, and was generally . . . happy. As far as I could see, he was happy in that present moment, his excitement uncomplicated by regrets or burdens, at least any that I could see that afternoon.

Lucky him.

And I just keep hearing it.

Unless you become as little children . . .

～

The boys gobble their pastries and cookies, having been warned that this might well be lunch today, and then run off to the swings, the slide, and the climbing structure. They're blocked on the slides by two little girls who have commandeered the high platform as they sit right in the middle of it chatting, just like little girls anywhere.

Katie points out a small extended family across the way. There's an older man, a young couple, a baby in a stroller, and a little boy dressed, not in Pokémon, but another international icon—Spider-Man—from head to toe.

Not only is Spider-Man enjoying the heights of Mussomeli, but someone else is, too. It's not Sciascia, not even Padre Pio, but even better, it's the pope! John Paul II, as big as life, stands on a pedestal at the entrance to the park. From what I can make out on the plaque, though, he never actually set foot in Mussomeli, much less this particular playground, but he'd sent some blessings along with someone else.

It gets to be about two in the afternoon, and we've had our fun up here in the park, but in order to see anything more in Mussomeli, we'll have to wait at least two more hours for churches and stores to open back up. We'll just move on.

~

To where? I think. Sutera perhaps? Sutera is yet another hill town, and it's not that far away. I can see it as I drive down from Mussomeli and pass the castle one last time. Sutera sits on top of a rise that's so steep, I can't imagine the road that would take you to the top. I had wanted to go there; it was on my list for today, and as the crow flies, it's not very far: about ten kilometers, but we know what that means.

And do you know what else? I'm tired.

Tired of the winding, hairpin turns. Tired of things taking so much longer than I expect. Tired of the real distance being farther than it looks on paper. Tired of trying to figure out the best way from one moment to the next, the most entertaining site, what will be open or closed, of how everyone's feeling and what, right now, they can cheerfully put up with. Tired of trying to discern the meaning of it all.

"How about we just go back and swim?" I suggest.

~

As we pull into the dirt parking space in front of the farmhouse, and before we can change, Claudia greets us with an offer. She and Marco would like to take us on a tour of the farm, so we jump from one car into another, all piling into their banged-up station wagon, Michael on my lap, and Marco drives us around the fields and groves. They show us the almond trees and the olives, point-ing out the difference between the older growth and the new, talking about their plans for the future of the farm.

We reach the fields that spread along the road leading to the farm's gate, and as Claudia explains, I finally understand some-thing that has puzzled me for these past few days.

On one side of this road leading to the agriturismo the fields are neatly cultivated. The wheat grows in clearly defined rows that sweep up and down the hills, bounded by shrubbery and trees, leading into vineyards and groves on either side. On the other side of a long hedge, a man on a motor scooter herds a flock of sheep. It's a tidy scene.

But on Claudia's side of the road, it just looks simply like an unkempt random field of yellowish grass. Except it's not, I'm learning. Since the farm is organic and they don't use pesticides or weed killers, the wheat and the chickpeas grow side by side with the weeds, to be separated at the harvest.

. . . *He replied, "No, if you pull up the weeds you might uproot the wheat along with them. Let them grow together until harvest."* . . . *(Mt. 13:29–30)*

I could never envision what Jesus was talking about before. That is, I could never envision it in the literal sense, so here it is. But harmful weeds and good wheat, growing in a jumble, so dif-ficult to separate? I know what that looks like. It's where I live, it's where I'm standing right now, in every sense.

I'm surrounded by parables, I realize. On one side of me, sheep and their shepherd, on the other, weeds and the wheat growing together, brushing up against each other, roots intertwining, from a distance so difficult to separate out, but not difficult for the One who harvests and who also shepherds, who sees *celebrate*, who sees *died*, who sees *life*, who sees *death* and knows exactly what it all means, even if I don't.

After some pool time, I ask Claudia for a dinner recommendation, and she points us to Il Cacciatore on Highway 640, just up the road, south of Caltanissetta.

Now, this is Italy, and furthermore it is southern Italy, and I know full well that no one eats dinner at six. They don't eat dinner at seven, either. The ideal is nine, but there's no way this crew can wait more than three hours for dinner, even with snacks. I put it off for as long as I can—and so we arrive at the restaurant, with its copious outdoor seating—perhaps two dozen tables under a canopy—at 8:15.

Alone.

Of course.

I'm coming to believe I have a future as a tour guide for what I'm going to call "Sicily for Introverts."

So it's awkward, and I ask, to make sure, that it's not a bother for us to be there, and I am assured that it's not.

Later Claudia tells me that the restaurant folks can always tell when their customers are Americans from her agriturismo, because they're the people standing awkwardly at the door some time before nine o'clock.

More customers arrive around that time, near the end of our very good meal—including a couple of families with young children. Things are clearly starting to pick up about 9:30, but by then it's time for us to go. I always wonder about that, seeing kids up so late in Europe. Not the same way I wonder about seeing little kids being dragged through Walmart at 10:30 at night, but still, I do wonder.

～

That night, after the children have gone to bed, I sit outside and talk to Claudia, who is sitting at a table near the pool, working on her little netbook, which is exactly like mine, except hers is white. She tells me the story of how she and her husband came from Palermo to run the farm, which had been her father's. She talks about her decision to go organic, and of her experience of being a woman in a business dominated by men. We talk about business and store hours in Sicily and she confesses to being inconvenienced and annoyed herself, as a businesswoman needing to meet with different professionals, go to the bank, and so on, at places not being open when it was convenient, especially since every different type of business seems to run on different hours.

I try to explain how it's different in America. I tell her that when my children were babies, and, say, I ran out of diapers at midnight, even though it's midnight, any day of the week, I can probably go somewhere within a mile of my house, where I can buy diapers. At midnight.

She is astonished, and while we agree this was a convenience, I can't brag about it too much, for in the telling, it just doesn't seem right. Doesn't seem right for someone to have to pull the midnight shift so I can pick up some diapers I was too stupid to plan for earlier in the day. Claudia points out that it's a job, at least, and she's right about that.

I tell her about our day, about the castle, about the park in Mussomeli with the statue of the pope. She remembers the day, years ago, when she stood in the fields, holding her infant daughter in her arms as a helicopter carrying John Paul II flew over her standing in the field, the weeds and the wheat growing together, the sheep grazing across the road.

I waved, she says. *I'm sure he saw me.*

It was 1993, and he had read the riot act to the Mafia down in Agrigento.

He was a great man, she says, *such a man of God*.

We talk about Mike and how he died and what life was like and why I am here in Sicily. Why I think I am here, at least. She tells me about an experience she'd had after her father died, when she felt very clearly and strongly his permission and encouragement to take on the farm and make it what she dreamed.

Maybe, she says, *your idea to come here—maybe it wasn't just your idea. Maybe it was your husband's, too.*

She nods, certain.

Me, I'm not so sure. It's all mixed up for me right now: present, past, good, the bad, high-minded motives and selfish ones, tragedy and blessing, smiling faces and private pain. Standing in my own field of weeds and wheat, I confess as I habitually do—to myself at least—these days: I just don't know.

18

THE NORWEGIAN IS FURIOUS. I AM FRUSTRATED MYSELF, but really, I'm no match for the Norwegian.

"The only thing these people are professional about," he fumes as he strides away from the group of indifferent jeep drivers lounging in their shelter, "is taking your money!"

Lava rock crunches under our feet, up here in the damp clouds as I follow him into the warm café high on the slope of Mount Etna.

⤚

Sicilians call her Mother, and you can see Mother Etna from much of eastern Sicily, more or less, depending on the weather. I tell the kids as we drive over on Wednesday morning that she's called "Mother" because she gives life. She explodes, things die because of it, but then life emerges from that new, rich soil.

I've never seen a real volcano myself, but soon I will. I'll see what I'm preaching about: this life sprouting from destruction. Hard to believe that can happen, but they say it does. Hard to believe that what comes out of the hot chaos raining down is not only good soil for that new life, but apparently the best there is.

⤚

The drive from the farm over to Mount Etna is less than two hours, or might take more. To be sure we are sustained along the way, I stop at an autogrill that's very American-looking and even bears the name "On the Run: Fast, Fresh, Friendly." I've seen other businesses with English-language names: A "Penny Market" up in Mussomeli yesterday, as well as the "Fun Train," a music-blasting trolley bus zipping around Piazza Armerina on Sunday, overflowing with singing, waving, and laughing older Italians obviously fulfilling the train's mission. So that's what English communicates here: fast, cheap, and fun? We could do worse, I think.

The highway is smooth, I turn my headlights on for the tunnels, and on the way, Vulcan comes up. Katie's reading aloud from the guidebook as I drive, and one of the fun facts she tells us about Mount Etna is that legend and myth identified it as Vulcan's forge. The boys know all about Vulcan, the Roman god of fire, because they see him almost every day at home.

He stands high on Red Mountain in the middle of Birmingham, one arm outstretched, holding an arrow he's just fashioned. If you drive up (or down) Interstate 65 through the city, you'll see him as you pass, just like I did for the first time many years ago, sometime in the late 1990s. Mike and I sped through Birmingham one July afternoon in the middle of a strange road trip the summer before the fall he ended up getting engaged to someone who wasn't me and moving to California and before I got fed up with teaching and decided to give writing a serious shot.

The trip wasn't planned as a cemetery tour, but turned out to be just that: we visited Walker Percy's grave in Louisiana, then saw Elvis in Memphis, Thomas Merton in Kentucky, then back down south, just past Birmingham, took in Hank Williams in Montgomery. It was all about tombs and graves, that trip, and on the way, we just passed through Birmingham. I remembering seeing the Vulcan and the city surrounded by mountains, but then I forgot it, never imagining at the time that years from then, I would be living there, with Mike because we had ended up married, but then without him, because Mike would be lying in his own grave.

So, Vulcan. He's the largest cast-iron statue in the world, and he was Birmingham's proud contribution to the 1904 World's Fair in St. Louis. After the fair, he was returned to the top of Red Mountain, where he has been standing vigil for over a century now. We see Vulcan all the time. Whenever I turn a corner or drive over a rise that brings me in sight of him—which is now every morning as I drive the boys to school, a task that used to be his—I hear Mike.

"*There he is, brothers!*" he'd announce as Vulcan appeared.

And the boys would giggle and point because Vulcan, you see, doesn't wear any pants.

There he is!

⁓

Since Vulcan's forge over here on the other side of the world is vast, there are naturally any number of approaches to the ascent. Most convenient to us is the southern route, which will take us through the town of Nicolosi, then on a drive up the mountain to a tourist area about fourteen hundred meters below the summit, then six hundred meters more on a gondola, and finally, if the weather cooperates, close to the top on minibuses to the craters where some of the real live volcano action is.

Driving to Mount Etna strikes me as being somewhat like traveling from California to far northern new England in the space of a little more than an hour. We're driving from the farm eastward, passing through yellowish-brown fields in between exposed craggy rocks for a while. We might glimpse the sea, and then we turn and start to climb, and as we rise, the world changes around us, quickly.

The dusty beige soil turns into the richest of black, great clumps mixed with shades of reds, greens, and browns, metals thrown up from deep below. The scrubby bushes and grasses disappear and conifers take over, pine trees surround us, and pink, white, and purple flowers blossom in the blackness.

We've got a thermometer in the car, so the boys (and the girls,

I'll admit) keep their eyes on it, calling out the temperature as it sheds degrees. By the time we stop, we're fifteen degrees cooler than when we started.

The road we're on is new and sweeps graciously up the mountain. The world is changing around us, and it's a dramatic change, but the road makes the way up through the changes almost effortless.

Before we know it, we are in the clouds.

~

Cool air chills us when we get out of the car at the Rifugio Sapienza, the large strip of souvenir and equipment shops that surrounds a parking lot, with a hotel across the way. It's a tidy, clean patch of structures with an alpine feel, planted on the side of this mountain, surrounded by the blackest soil I have ever seen. Yes, we're shivering in our short sleeves, but there's a plan for that. Seriously. This time, there's a plan. After all, why consume luggage space with jackets when you can buy one on the spot when you need it and also get a souvenir in the process? When it comes to souvenirs, I usually go for either the tacky or the useful. If I hit the jackpot—both.

The souvenir shops have plenty of useful gear, but they also have the useless and tacky. The mementos and kitsch, figurines large and small, are purportedly fashioned out of lava rock, which doesn't surprise me (even as I doubt the truth of it), but what does surprise me is all the glitter.

The lion's mane, the birds' beaks, the rabbits' tails all sparkle. They line the shelves, outlined and filled in with blue, green, and gold. I let the boys each pick one, and Joseph immediately grabs a dragon holding a golden ball in its claws. Michael, though, is not taken in by the glitter that is not gold, and he instead fixates on a cheap plastic faux camera with a kind of View-Master thing going on inside. He adores it, he begs for it, I buy it for him, and he then spends the rest of the vacation taking many, many photos with it, all of which end up looking exactly like Mount Etna. Go figure.

Me, I'm fixated too, but by the religious figurines. The Virgin, Pope John II, Padre Pio! All black but for a blue shimmery veil, a sparkly green coating on Pio's robe, red accents on the pope's robes. I think it's all pretty great, I'm amused, and then I'm hit by the familiar twinge that turns, fast, into a kick in the gut, and I have to turn away.

Strange how a Jesus wearing a glittery red loincloth, outlined in gold hanging on a lava rock crucifix can make you miss your husband more than anything.

~

After I get red fleece jackets with a simple stitched mountain and MOUNT ETNA for the boys and Katie finds a white hoodie with SICILIA emblazoned across the front, we decide to eat before we go up on the funicular. The restaurant is around the bend of the shops, and it's got that mountain theme going on, of course, in a brown exterior edged in scalloping white trim. It's a cafeteria with a crew of cheerful, friendly fellows on the line who speak a little English and who point the boys to some chicken cutlets, protein that they do really need. They devour them, and then ask for more, along with some pasta and fruit. Katie takes some pasta, and I'm more than content with an antipasto plate that is piled high with preserved and marinated vegetables. It's gorgeous. It's fantastic. I'm shocked at how great the food is. It will be one of the best meals we had on our trip—no kidding, right up there on Mount Etna.

A table of Germans sit near us. A television loops programming about the formation and history of the volcano—it's in Italian, but still the little boys, deprived of television for a week now, sit slack-jawed after they've finished eating, staring at the box like starving men, uncertain of the mirage in front of them.

❧

The fellow at the gondola office warns me against buying a ticket for the ascent following this one, the one that would go to the highest level of the volcano. He says the weather is too uncertain, and there are no refunds for tickets, so I take his advice and just buy us a passage on this, yet another capsule swinging through the air.

As we ride up, that destructive, life-giving blackness spreads beneath us. We rise, and it rises up with us, blanketing Mother Etna's side. Some of the dark earth is slick, a solidified lava flow, but most of it lies in crumbling soil and chunks of rock tossed from the middle of the earth in some previous explosion. Colors sprout between crevices and out of rocks. We see green and red, we see pink, we see yellow scattered through the blackness like glitter.

Far below us, hikers make their way up the slope. I see a group of three pause in their hike and look back behind them. I follow the direction of their gaze and see the straggler, who looks to me like he only has an inch to go until he reaches his friends.

❧

About two weeks after Michael died, I found myself surprised. I was surprised because as I prayed—prayed the Mass, the Liturgy of the Hours, the rosary—none of the words of any of those prayers included phrases like:

Oh, God, bring Michael back

or

God of Heaven and Earth, let Amy go back in time and forcibly take Michael to the doctor

or

The Third Glorious Mystery: Time is transcended, Michael has his cell phone on him, and Amy is contacted immediately instead of five hours after it happened.

or even

Blessed be God, let Amy feel Michael's presence.

I didn't hear or read any of that, anywhere.

Instead it was all about God.

God here, God there. Thirsting for God's presence, for God's love and justice. Rejoicing, even. Rejoicing in the Word made flesh, embracing the cross. Mercy was sought. Mercy was begged for. Peace. Refuge from enemies. Eyes looking forward, hearts aching, spirits racing for God.

I was tempted to dismiss it all out of hand. *Who needs that crap*, I thought. *Mike died. We have a crisis here.* I regret to say I probably did. Dismiss the prayers that, oddly enough, did not mention my life, that is.

Another night a couple of weeks later, I sat on the floor with the rosary he carried in his pocket, the other hand resting on that shadow box full of relics, and probably a shirt of his near at hand. All right, I'll admit it. A shirt of his on my body, enveloping me with that scent. And even though I knew he would be saying, "Are you *nuts*?" at the sight, I thought, *If I do this, I will feel close to him. It will be like we are just sitting on the couch watching* Big Love.

That's how I was praying that night, and that's what I was praying for—to live in a world with Mike living in it again—and in the middle of the decades of the rosary, the truth shot back at me, a voice so strong to be unmistakable, not from my own imagination, but from without, so strong it almost knocked me over.

"Seek God," it said, "not Michael."

Mike prayed. He prayed the Office almost the last twenty-five years or so. Prayed the rosary every day for longer. Went to Mass every day that he was able, which was most of them.

I'd been praying—or pretending to pray—those prayers he prayed rather intensely, more intensely than I ever had over the past few weeks. As I prayed there surrounded by his praying stuff, I thought about Mike thumbing through his prayer books, reading those words, lifting his eyes to the icons and crucifixes around him, and then praying them again and again, for years.

My being thirsts for God, the living God. . . . When can I go and see the face of God? . . . Thy will be done on earth, as it is in heaven. . . . My heart and flesh cry out for the living God. . . . For in this tent we groan, longing to be further clothed with our heavenly habitation . . . At present I know partially; then I shall know fully, as I am fully known. . . . Now, Master, you let your servant go in peace.

It hit me with great force as, for the first time in weeks, I managed to shut myself up and actually listen to what I was saying.

I listened to the words of the Psalmist, of Paul, of Simeon, and through them all, the voice of Jesus coursed as well: *unless a grain of wheat shall die.* I listened, and didn't hear it as a metaphor this time. I heard it as a fact. If I'm going to pray for salvation, redemption, and God's embrace, I have to be ready to die.

Mike prayed for all that. He prayed for salvation, redemption, and God's embrace.

Those prayers that he prayed all his life?

They've been answered, I realized.

In the only way they can.

~

The gondola capsule deposits us into a café, equipment, and souvenir shop high on the mountainside. It's a tight squeeze with only about six tables, but a couple dozen of us wait in here to proceed farther up the mountain in one of the minibuses parked on the other side of the wall of windows.

I head to the register to buy tickets for the ride farther up. No sale. The weather, the young woman claims, has gone bad, so they probably would not be going up anymore today. *Probably*, she says, but she doesn't shut the door completely, so for the next thirty minutes I walk back and forth between this woman, who speaks a little English and the drivers standing around outside, who speak none, trying to get a straight story.

At first the woman in the café says she won't sell me a ticket until she hears from her "colleague" outside. That's fair. So I trudge outside to report this to the colleague in the tent by the buses, who only repeats that he really can't discuss this with me until I've bought a ticket. Inside the café. I keep trying to tell him that inside won't sell me a ticket until she hears from him that it is all a go. Back and forth, back and forth, until finally, the bus drivers draw covers over the turnstiles, turn their backs, and huddle under the shelter for a smoke.

Too bad, but not a terrible problem. Katie and the boys have spent their time climbing a bit farther up on their own (you could do so if you were able and wanted to), poking around in the lava rock, marveling at its colors, and then retiring to gelato. I've not built up the final ascent anyway, knowing the unpredictability of it all. Smoking craters would have been fun to see, but this is satisfying, too, so no one is devastated or even angry. Except, of course, the Norwegian.

~

Other, less lively craters would have to satisfy us. After we've been taken back down on the gondola, we drive out of the parking lot and see the sign for Silvestri Craters, which, although not churning with hot life from underground, are actually pretty impressive holes in the ground. Just empty holes, yes, but deep, vast hundreds of meters wide and dozens deep filled with lava rock, bright flowers, and places to climb, edges to master, many, many brilliantly colored rocks. The rocks crunch under our feet. I crouch down and examine the vegetation that's growing here, the strong little plants, the perfect blooms that spring to life because other things have died.

The rocks are small, the rocks are large, but because they are made of lava and are porous, they are really not what they seem. They look like they would be far too heavy to raise from the ground, but it's just not so. A child can pick up one of these rocks that's five times the size of his head, and not only get it off the ground, but he can hoist it high, laughing.

I'll take that picture, yes, and I'll print it out so I'll remember what the eight-year-old boy in the red jacket looked like when he stood down there at the bottom of that pit blasted out of the side of Vulcan's forge.

There he is, grinning, mastering the thing that looks as though it should crush him. But it won't, because ultimately this giant piece of earth is not what it seems. Like death. Like life.

19

CLAUDIA IS PLEASED BECAUSE, AT LAST, WE ARE GOING to Cefalù.

Every morning she has asked us, hopefully, if we will be going to Cefalù that day. She keeps telling me that Cefalù—a popular beach town to the north, east of Palermo—is wonderful, that we will certainly like it very much. I keep telling her that since the last part of our Sicily sojourn—which begins Friday, which is tomorrow—involves a B and B that is (I think) actually *on a beach*, I'm not *that* interested in beach time right now, and I think I would like to try to fit the nearby city of Enna in instead. She is undeterred, reminding me about the duomo, which she's certain I'll find interesting to compare to that in Monreale. And there is the town, which she tells me we will enjoy because there are many things to do and see.

So she is delighted on Thursday morning when I tell her that yes, today, we will be going to Cefalù. I'm really not sure why I've decided this except that as interesting as Enna sounds, in reading about it, I couldn't quite grasp a central purpose to it. I couldn't focus the day in my head. Cefalù was a little farther away, but the concept of it seemed simpler on a day when my mind was already looking ahead, preparing for packing up and moving on to the next place: compare Pantocrator in duomo to same in Monreale; beach; gelato. Got it. Easy enough.

Or, you could say she just wore me down and I finally gave in to peer pressure. Either one.

On the way north to Cefalù, a fight breaks out in the backseat. It's the worst fight of the trip, an explosion over the video game, of course. There are serious tears and accusations and resentments, and as he tends to do when upset—for whatever reason—Joseph wails, "*I want Daddy!*"

I'm sure he does, but right then, at that moment, I honestly doubt that Mike is on his mind. I've suspected for a time that there are moments—rare, but present—in which Joseph turns this on almost like an excuse, a rationalization, a distraction, a deflection. As in—*I'm acting badly, I deserve to be punished or reprimanded, but I'll pull the Daddy card and maybe get off this time.*

I tentatively asked our counselor about this. I hated to seem like a total, unfeeling heel, but I had my suspicions. She wasn't shocked, and in fact she nodded. "It happens," she assured me.

The thing is, I get it. I totally sympathize, because it happens to me, too. If I don't feel like cleaning or writing or shuffling papers and can't rouse myself to do anything but surf the Internet or stare into space, chaos building around me, I can pull out the Mike card, even if I'm talking to no one but myself.

My husband died four months ago. Come on. What do you expect me to do?

It's even in my mental file for any possible future screwups regarding taxes or bills or such.

I'm so sorry—I just couldn't think straight for a while. My husband died. Suddenly. Can I just write you a check now?

So, yes, I understand the Daddy card, and I am almost sure Joseph is pulling it at this moment, but that's okay.

It's okay because the Daddy card isn't really a distinct thing anyway. The boy is, indeed, more agitated, more stressed, on edge because his father never came home that day in February. So sure, when he does lash out, what he says is perfectly, absolutely true.

He does so want Daddy.

There in the car, trying to bring things back to calm, I answer the way I usually do, despite knowing that there are other things that I probably should be saying that would point him to higher truths and more self-control. No, right now, driving my kids by myself to the beach, I say what I think and no more:

Me too.

~

There's certainly a lot to like about Cefalù, I'll give Claudia that much. Crowded between the Mediterranean and a huge, jutting plateau of rock called, appropriately, "La Rocca," it's a cramped, busy tourist town, with the heaviest traffic I've navigated since Palermo. I attempt to follow a sign pointing to the centro and the duomo, but I'm stopped. A policewoman strides toward us and waves her arms: *No, no, no!* She picks up that I'm American and tells me in English that no cars are allowed in the centro.

"So how do I get to the duomo?" I ask.

She looks at me.

"You *walk*."

Oh, of course. *Grazie. Scusi.*

I turn us around and head for the beach area, which is just a few blocks away. Cefalù is crowded today and the beach looks like it's wall-to-wall people, but despite that, a parking place opens up on the street along the beach. I grab it, we get out, lock the car, and we all search up and down the street, scrutinize every sign. I can't imagine for a moment that this prime spot is free, but none of us can find even the slightest hint of how it's to be paid for: no meters, no central, slotted money box . . . nothing. I'll take the risk and leave it, although if it turns out badly, I'll be out of luck because I'm pretty sure the Mike card isn't going to help me make my case.

~

Here in the Cefalù duomo, the modesty police are out and they have snagged me at last.

You don't stroll into an Italian church dressed any way you please. Everyone knows that, especially all those North African fellows strategically selling scarves and wraps just outside St. Peter's Square in Rome.

And me, I don't travel in shorts anyway. *You're welcome.* My uniform is a skirt and some sort of T-shirt top or shell. But today—well, today, I didn't think, except that it was hot and we were going to the beach, so along with the skirt, over my swimsuit, I pulled on a tank top, so now me and my bare shoulders are stopped short at the entrance to the duomo in Cefalù and I am handed a shabby salmon-colored shawl, for which I get the privilege of donating a euro or two.

My daughter is ecstatic at the judgment. She, the object of years of nagging about skirt length, can't stop laughing, and I don't blame her. Schadenfreude is, indeed, pretty sweet.

~

Wrapped in my shawl and glad it's not black so I'm not too much of a stereotype huddled here in the church pew in Italy, I sit behind a tour group being lectured about this duomo of Cefalù.

They're Germans. Since I, let me remind you, am not German, I don't understand the tour guide. So I read my *Blue Guide* in the dim light, and I learn that the duomo was built a few decades before the one in Monreale. It bears its own array of beautiful eastern-flavored mosaics: the apostles, rather than the complete cycle of salvation history, predominate here in the sanctuary. The walls in the tall nave itself, however, are mostly bare. They were redecorated in the baroque period, in, presumably a baroque style, so in order to re-create a sense of the original structure, those later, more elaborate features were stripped away. It seems that devotion to authenticity only goes so far, though, since the replacement stained glass is composed of bland, geometric abstracts that don't fit at all.

The angels are, just like those in Monreale, hovering with their Navajo wings. Jesus the Pantocrator here is different from that in Monreale. A lock of hair falls over his forehead as it does there, but it is more predominant and almost seems more random, more askew. Jesus's stern look is considerably softened here and he looks aside, almost concerned. There's scaffolding in the sanctuary. The Germans crane their necks and study the apostles. I try to catch Jesus's eye, me sitting in my shawl in between the cold bare walls. I wonder what he's so worried about.

~

We spend a pleasant afternoon wandering Cefalù. We find the quirky Museo Mandralisca, where we study the eclectic private collection of art, antiquities, antiques, and (best of all for some of us) stuffed animal specimens—a bobcat in a case, teeth bared, ready to strike; birds affixed on the walls; a porcupine, quills ablaze, glass eyes glaring at us.

Outside the museum, we watch workmen repairing cobblestones, along with about ten others, gathered around, pointing, commenting, giving advice. A few blocks down, Katie gets a lemon and cherry gelato sandwich for lunch; after we pay, I decide I'll go ahead and get the rest of us something in this same place, but then a screaming match breaks out in the street, and two guys are striding quickly toward each other, yelling, arms waving, so we move on.

After an hour or so of just seeing the town, Michael taking frequent photos in which Cefalù will look surprisingly like Mount Etna, Joseph sketching in his notebook, we return to where we left our car, where it's supposed to be right there on the street near the beach—

—and it is.

This Cefalù beach is much more crowded than the one at San

Vito Lo Capo, but as I settle into my rented chair in the midst of the sunning throngs, it looks to me as if the exact same vendors have simply worked their way east from there. The guys with their poles strung with plastic toys. The Asian women carting tables about, selling massages. Towels, hats, and jewelry. *Pursa prego. Bella pursa prego! Coco-coco-coco nuts!*

The tourists are from everywhere. Need I specify Germans? Well, they're here. Next to me, a woman is absorbed in a German translation of a Lee Child novel. An Italian man on the other side of me reads *Quattroruote*—a car magazine. A Frenchman leafs through *Le Monde*. There's a large family group of Russians just a bit farther down the beach, but still close enough to hear— grandparents and a couple with two children, and the mother is pregnant. No Russian birth dearth here. They are loud and enthusiastic and boisterous and I think—they are what people say American tourists are like.

La Rocca towers behind us, over the town. Netting is fastened in places, holding back falling rock.

Kayakers glide over the flat sea.

Katie falls asleep on the chair beside me. A vendor comes by with purses, I tell him no, but he keeps right on talking. Michael, digging in the sand next to me, looks up at him and says, very loudly, *"Noooooooooo!"*

His back bending under the load of purses, the vendor trudges on.

Of course I can see him, as if he were here, which he wouldn't be even if he were alive, since Sicily wasn't on his bucket list, but I see him anyway. Maybe someday I'll stop trying to, but not today. He would be in his swim trunks, a Marlins or Gators baseball cap—and sunglasses. He would be well covered in sunscreen and would have meticulously covered the boys in the same, being sure to get their ears, which I always forget. He would have some book—probably on scripture or spirituality or maybe something by Pope Benedict. He would read it sometimes, but more often than not, he would set the book down on his knee and look around, chugging from a water bottle. He would comment on the Russians and file them in his repertoire. He would pick up his book, adjust his cap, crack a joke in a Russian accent, or if he was reading Benedict intone *Fratelli e sorelle* and start reading again.

But he's not doing that. He's not here.

He's not in the apartment back home, he's not in his office, he's not in the midst of his family—us or his parents and sisters.

What am I supposed to make of that? I know, I know. *Alleluia*. Right.

~

I'm trying. Well, if you define "thinking about him all the time and feeling guilty about it" as trying—yes, I'm trying. I have high standards to live up to in my very interesting Catholic family of saints, the people I'm supposed to emulate. Take St. Augustine, for example. When his mother, St. Monica, died, Augustine mourned. For a day or two, that is. He suppressed his tears at first, but then, the day after her funeral, gave in. He wept—for an hour. An hour, he gave himself, and even then, that sorrow he offered to God, and as he writes of it in his *Confessions*, he seems somewhat abashed, anticipating reproach, and begs the reader not to laugh at him.

I feel as if I should be there. I know it, in fact. But I'm continually tripped up by the simple fact that I miss him a lot. Jesus looked worried back there in the duomo. Sitting there on the beach, trying to live in the present, trying not to imagine Mike next to me, I think of how I engaged this battle as I dealt with the things he left behind.

Mike's clothes and other possessions, from the icons to the Warren Zevon albums, represented both ends of the equation to me, both possibilities of judgment. If I cleaned out the closets, drawers, and boxes so soon, what was I saying? If I hung on to them . . . what was I saying?

Not that my decisions about his personal effects would make the papers, not that anyone was watching. I wasn't blogging or tweeting about it on Twitter or making a big deal about it to anyone, especially the kids. It was basically just between me and the stuff.

Which meant it was between me and him, of course. Because that's all that was left.

Which is why, with every shirt I gave up, every book I packed, every CD I placed in the "give away" pile, I felt that an apology was in order.

So I did. Over and over again, I said it, sorry about everything, crying.

I'm sorry. I'm so sorry. I am so, so sorry, Michael.

And I knew he'd forgive me, because I knew that if the roles were reversed, he'd be doing the same thing. He wouldn't cling or construct a museum to me. He might even be pissed off at all the stuff I was leaving with him to deal with. And after he shook that off, he'd do exactly what I was doing: keep a few items of clothing that were pure him, that were good, strong relics—sports hats and shirts, a shirt with palm trees on it that he wore a lot. For the boys, plastic bins of a representative sample of his books and CDs, with a note from me, for them, for the future, about how David Allen Coe, Warren Zevon, and Orthodox chant and Archbishop Fulton Sheen and Pope Benedict XVI explain their father. A bit. They explain him a bit.

Files, of course, his papers, journals, letters, photographs stayed. I've got all that. They'll explain even more. A bit more.

The books and CDs that didn't interest me I gave to the parish rummage sale. There was even a surfeit of icons and prayer and devotional books—quite a bit of duplication in the latter. How many different versions of the Bible, of the Catechism, how many different kinds of prayer book do I really need? I asked a

Catholic prison chaplain if he could use them. He said yes, so off they went, to the prisoners.

The clothing I passed on to a men's mission in town that serves recovering alcoholics and addicts, men who've lost their way. When I unloaded my car there, and the men on the loading dock took bag after bag, suits on hangers, dress shirts and ties, I wondered if they were wondering why the not-young but not-very-old woman was unloading all of this. So of course I had to explain, didn't I? I looked up them as they took the last black plastic trash bag out of my hands and I was going to say more, but all I could manage was, "My husband died," before I rushed back into the car and drove away.

Not all of it went then, though. I held some back, for a while.

He did his own laundry, and he only washed his dress shirts every two or three wearings. So even when I return from Sicily, there will be a tight row of work shirts waiting for me that still, after almost six months, bear his scent, the mix of his body, his deodorant and his cologne—both Paul Sebastian. They hang there and still, when I am home, whenever I want, if I am near, even knowing the folly, knowing that I should be thinking finer, more eternal thoughts, humming *Alleluia* as I walk by an empty closet, I pause at the closet that's not quite empty and take in what's left.

No one's watching, everyone's watching, he's watching. I don't care. I am weak. For a moment, two stories aboveground, in a place I never thought I would be, trying not to make idols, trying to really love, to hope for his eternal hope, but still, I can't help but gather them all in close. My face in his shirts.

Buried.

20

FRIDAY, MIDMORNING, CLAUDIA AND I ARE SETTLING accounts. It's been a great week, and the boys are already asking about a return trip (not impossible, and something I would also like, but maybe simply buying a dog would be cheaper), but today's our day to move on to the southeastern coast for some more beach time.

Claudia has a question for me before we go, after I've given her the Cefalu report and thanked her for sending us there.

"What does"—she pauses and studies the screen of her netbook sitting open on the dining room table—"*highlight* mean?"

"Oh, it means the best. You go somewhere and the best experience you have is the highlight."

She smiles, a bit shyly. "A Canadian who stayed here, he wrote to me and said this was the *highlight* of his trip. So that's good?"

Yes. It's very good. The best.

～

We don't actually drive away until around noon. I had tossed one more load of laundry in the wash, afraid that we wouldn't have the chance again until we get to Barcelona next Wednesday (I was right), but had started the load later than I should have and the Sicilian sun didn't burn as warmly as I hoped.

But eventually we get away. Katie jumps out of the car at the bottom of the hill to close and lock the gate one more time behind us. The car bumps along the dirt road past the vineyards, the almond and olive trees, between the neat rows of a stranger's wheat on the right and our friend Claudia's messy mix of weeds and wheat on the left.

A week ago, this was uncharted territory, but now it feels like we're leaving home. We're quiet as the fields, the groves, and the vineyards fall behind us. I miss it already. The next place I'm going is more mysterious, but I hope that the same thing will happen there: that I'll get to know it, I'll adapt, and the unknown will end up feeling like somewhere I belong. I hope.

So what did I know about our next destination, about where I'm taking us today? Well, the B and B in Cava d'Aliga on the southeastern coast does have a website and even an English-language version. Paolo, whose picture was on this website and whom I assumed owned the property, answered my e-mails promptly in excellent English.

But what made me nervous was that I couldn't find any reviews of the place online, not in English, not in any language. That part of Sicily is known for its flat, expansive beaches, but also known for them by hardly anyone but Italians, which is great with me, but also leaves me a little in the dark. The B and B—which attracted me in part with photos of tables laid out for breakfast under a canopy of trees—is supposedly in walking distance from the beach. The photos looked good, the satellite views don't reveal great heaps of trash or oil refineries nearby, so it didn't seem as if we'll be descending into either filth or an orgiastic den of a Sicilian Club Med. I think we'll be okay. We'll go to the beach, we'll listen to people speaking Italian, we'll take in some of the baroque-styled towns that corner of the island is known for, we'll relax for a few days, until we return the car and fly from Catania to Barcelona next Wednesday. It will be fine.

～

There is no absolutely direct route from the farm to Cava d'Aliga, but there is probably a more direct one than the one we're taking. I'll take the blame for this, since I was the only one who determined that since Caltagirone, one of the great Italian centers of ceramic arts was kind of, sort of on the way, we might as well check it out.

For you see, there are all these steps in Caltagirone: one hundred sixty-two of them, each riser decorated with pictures and designs in tile, steps that rise up a hill in the center of town (on a hill itself, naturally) up to the church of Santa Maria del Monte. I'd like to see it and think that little boys and almost two hundred steps seems like a fantastic combination for the middle of a travel day. We can probably get some Christmas shopping out of the way while we're at it, too. So we're all on board for this stop before the final destination, but an hour into the drive, I'm having second thoughts because I'm tired, and just as I was two days ago after we left Mussomeli, I'm fed up with roads turning back in on themselves, wrong turns, and U-turns.

I keep on though, partly because it's too late to turn back and take another way, but also because I do believe there's always something worth seeing. *Just wait*, I keep telling myself, as I swing around one more turn that seems to take me right back to where I was a minute ago, *something interesting will turn up soon*.

⤳

It's early afternoon, so of course the streets of this town we're passing through right now are empty, the windows are shuttered, and no one is about.

But here's something different: on this hot, sleepy Friday afternoon, I see doors to a fairly large church that are flung wide open. How strange, and how interesting, I think. This isn't normal, since the churches are shut up just as tightly as any shop during the reposa. I decide that I just want to peek and see what it's like, and that will take one-tenth as long if I leave everyone else in the car. They don't object. So I park on the street, grab the camera, dash up the steps, and step into the dark, cool interior.

What immediately catches my eye is not Padre Pio this time—although he must be around somewhere—but what seems to be a statue of St. Nicholas up to the right of the altar. Nicholas has ties to southern Italy—his relics are in Bari, on the eastern tip, but I'm still surprised to see him in a Sicilian church. Perhaps I shouldn't be, but I am.

I start up the aisle, still in a hurry, my eyes fixed on who I think might be St. Nicholas, when I'm stopped in my tracks by the reason the church is open here in the middle of the day:

A casket.

Closed, but still a casket there in the center aisle right in front of me. A dozen more steps forward, and I could touch it. No one waits with it, no one watches. It lies there alone in the church. Someone was alive last week, and now his or her corpse is lying inside that box settling into itself, waiting to blessed, waiting for the Paschal candle to be lit, waiting to be lowered into the ground, to be changed.

I don't take any pictures. I don't look for Padre Pio. I just turn around and race down the steps back to the car.

I tell Katie, *sub voce*, what I'd seen in the church. She shivers, we chuckle, and since that's all I say to her about it, it's just a funny, eerie, story. The boys look out the window at the empty streets, waiting to move on, wanting to climb all those steps I've been telling them about.

～

I find the way out of town. I am the kind of person who, if you ask me what date it is, I have to stop and think about it, and I usually need two tries to get it right. But I know what today is, have known all day, and have known since yesterday and the day before that. Speeding down the road away from this town, I remember the body in the church, and I continue to absorb the fact that today is the third of July. It's around two in the afternoon. It's five months to the day—and if you ignore the technicalities of time changes—it's just around the hour I stood in the emergency room and stared at my husband's dead body for the first time. Five months to the day and the hour, I practically bump into a coffin in the middle of Sicily.

All along, I've been saying that this trip wasn't about escaping, even if I did admit to myself that I was coming all this way, to this place without connection to me or to us to lessen the chances of being haunted.

Well, apparently what the Buddhists say is true: wherever you go, there you are.

It was silent in the church. The town outside was silent, stretching out to rest in cool shadows. For all I knew standing there, the casket in my sights, unable to see or hear anything but that moment, the whole world was silent as well. Astonished at God—for that is whom I blamed—for bringing me here at this time, on this day, to face another death, I prayed for their souls—both of them, all of them, all around the world and just departed from it. I prayed for all of us left behind, wondering how we got to this place, where we are supposed to go next.

~

So, no, I wouldn't have seen that. And if I'd taken a more direct route down to the coast, neither would we have seen a few other things. We wouldn't have seen a few cacti scattered by the side of the road, which then proceeded to get more organized and multiply until they surrounded us: acre after acre of sharp, green prickly pears. That was pretty great.

I wouldn't have had the triumph, of which I am stupidly proud, of my conversation with a gas station attendant a little north of Gela, in which using only my map, the word *dove*, and some creative arm waving, I was able to communicate to him the very important question, "Can you tell me just where the hell I am on this map and the fastest way to Cava d'Aliga from wherever this is?" And understood his answer!

We wouldn't have missed the turn that would have taken us around the town of Vittoria, which meant that we drove right through the middle of it instead, and did so at the height of the *passegiatta*, where the whole town seemingly awakened from the afternoon rest at the same time and hit the streets. I wouldn't have been crawling on those packed streets, frustrated at the slow, heavy traffic, wishing I'd been there an hour earlier, but also envious. I was sitting there at intersections, waiting for lights to change and the car ahead of me to just *move*, and so I had time to watch them out and about. Women with children by the hand shopped for their evening meal, men sat around outdoor tables (of course), teenagers roved in packs, divided, then joined up again, everyone chatted and hailed each other and kissed each other's cheeks.

A bride and groom, sitting in an open convertible, crossed at an intersection in front of us, waving. Everyone on the sidewalks paused and waved back.

All at once, it all made sense to me—the reposa, the passegiatta, the resting and the awakening, the refreshment, preparing for an evening meal, and it seemed no longer old-fashioned or inconvenient. I thought about my own busy American life *On the run* to the Penny Market in what was not always the Fun Train—of carpool and after-school activities and never-ending writing deadlines and scrambling, a life that never pauses until midnight and then picks right up again at 6:30 the next morning.

I sat there watching them all, thinking about this, and I was no longer so anxious to move on to the next place. I thought about how nice it would be to stop right there and just relax with them. How strangely wonderful it would be to take three—even four!—hours out of my day every day to just rest.

~

After the cactus but before Vittoria, we'd have missed Caltagirone—that is, if we'd not taken that indirect way that purposefully took us to Caltagirone. That would have been too bad, too, for those steps were something. Rising steeply in the middle of town, lined on each side by shops, ending at a (locked) church, they're beautiful, in the way the whole town is beautiful, alive with art and craft, swirling blues, greens, and yellows.

I think how every day on this trip seems to be about rocks or dirt or the earth in some way. We threw stones at the devils, we played in the sand, we rattled around in a castle of stone, dungeon and all, we tripped over volcanoes great and small, we studied gods in mosaic floors, God in glistening stone with that hair falling down his forehead, and here we kneel on steps, studying knights and castles and even a dragon or two painted onto mud, baked and lined on rising steps.

Michael is less interested in the array of images rising above him than climbing on them, so he does. He races, and Katie sticks close to his side, her hand outstretched behind his back. Joseph takes it at a slower pace, on his hands and knees like a penitent. He remarks on every castle, dragon, and knight that he spies. After enduring this drawn-out process for about twenty steps, I convince him to just walk the rest of the way up to the top.

Steep hills can trick you, for as you concentrate on how exhausting it is to climb up, you forget how treacherous the way down can be. The boys take the descent so freely, Katie and I stop them and insist that we'll walk ahead, so that at least they'll hit us, who are a bit softer than stone steps, on the way down. A group of Japanese tourists descend the steps ahead of us. The women are clinging to each other, and they can't stop laughing as they balance on the steep way down.

～

After a couple of hours of wandering, shopping, and gelato slurping, we make our way in a drizzle back to *Via Roma* and our car. We're carrying our packages of spoon rests, various animals, knights painted on tiles, a sweet little blue ceramic Vespa, decorative boxes, and I'm thinking how great it is to get that much

Christmas shopping out of the way. I'm also thinking how happy I am when I see my car parked where I left it.

Not so great? *My* present, left under the windshield wiper. Finally, a parking ticket.

In this week and a half, with no understanding of how to pay to park anywhere I've attempted it, there's the ticket I have probably deserved several times over. I really can't complain. I'm sure what I owe Sicily in parking fees and what Sicily is asking me to pay here probably evens out in the end. But I'm still irritated, as all of us, once again, search the street for some kind of sign or payment box or meter. We don't see anything, so I don't know what I should have done, except what I did.

So yes, if we'd taken the straight path, we'd have missed all that charm. We would have missed the prickly pears, the communicating, the communing, the beauty fashioned out of the earth, the treacherous way down from the heights, the parking ticket; we would have missed death that afternoon.

And what a shame that would have been.

～

I don't know anything much about heaven. I try not to think about it too much, because I'm so wary of falling into fantasy and wish fulfillment. But in the months after Mike's death, it was hard not to think about it, since I was always wondering where he was. In order to focus my thoughts, I decided to read some books.

Not books with fluffy clouds on the cover imaging who we'll meet and what we'll "do" in heaven written by people who didn't know anything more than I did. I hate those books. No, I needed some theology, so I pulled from what we had on hand, believing that if they were on our shelves, there was a reason, that they had something I was supposed to learn. I pulled out some N. T. Wright, Alexander Schmemann, St. Augustine, and Joseph Ratzinger and studied up on what they had to say about judgment, purgatory, heaven and hell, and eternity.

At the end of my reading course, I had learned a few things, but still didn't know much more than I did when I started, not because I am necessarily that dense (although I don't have a theological mind, that's true), but more because of the disconnect I was constantly feeling. I would read, take in a sentence, a paragraph, and while my eyes were still on the words on the page, it would almost make sense.

And then I would close the books, close my eyes, and think about him dead in his coffin, me dead in mine someday, and I would be confounded all over again. Confounded by picky questions of how we are saved body and soul if our bodies are disintegrating in the ground, what my prayers did for him in purgatory, what his prayers might do for us, wondering if he could see me and if I could talk to him, trying not to let my mind be blown by the minor thing called eternity.

What confused me most of all, though, was not the exact shape of heaven, and I eventually figured out that wasn't my question. To live in the perfect love of God, forgiven and known, is enough of a description for me. The destination, I get as much as I think I am allowed to.

No, what my confusion comes down to is that it would all be easier for me to understand if it were not for his body in the casket. I could even look at a photograph of the living Mike and connect him laughing with him living in God's love, somewhere, somehow. But then I would remember the still, lifeless, shrinking body, and get tripped up, and then get tripped up again by the coming fact of my own still, lifeless, shrinking body. Not that it scared me exactly, anymore. I just don't understand how we get from here to there, and I'm less sure of what the purpose of here is.

All those twists, turns, accidents, and things we see just because we're on the journey? Those, I don't understand. In other words, when I'd think about life with God, I'd think, *Sounds great. So why am I still here?* Because we sin and therefore we die may be the quick answer and even the correct one, but it doesn't quite answer it sufficiently.

I read all that theology, and it both reassured and confused me; about the same time, I rediscovered a prayer. An acquaintance who runs a Catholic goods company sent me a prayer book after Mike died, imprinted in his memory. The first time I opened it at Mass, after Communion, it fell open to the Anima Christi, a prayer I knew of, but didn't pay much attention to in the past. Now I did.

> Soul of Christ, sanctify me
> Body of Christ, save me
> Blood of Christ, inebriate me
> Water from Christ's side, wash me
> Passion of Christ, strengthen me
> O good Jesus, hear me
> Within Thy wounds hide me
> Suffer me not to be separated from Thee
> From the malicious enemy defend me
> In the hour of my death call me
> And bid me come unto Thee
> That I may praise Thee with Thy saints
> and with Thy angels
> Forever and ever.

So there it is, that body. I don't know if it's just a coincidence that I saw it that day or if it was put there on purpose and if on purpose, why. What I do know is that the body is there, the body confounds me, and the only answer that comes close to satisfying me is the one that I can't articulate in words, but comes, not in theory, but also in a body: the body on the crucifix, the body missing from the tomb, the Body of Christ.

Speaking of destinations, we got here. We got where we're going, to Cava d'Aliga in early evening, at least an hour later than I'd hoped. We're here, yes, but now it is late evening, almost the middle of the night, and everyone is asleep but me, and I am kneeling on my bed, computer balanced on the window ledge, trying to catch some Internet, working.

Working to see if I can get us out of here, to be someplace else, and do it tomorrow.

21

I T WASN'T THAT BIG OF A DEAL, REALLY, CERTAINLY NOT A tragedy, but it was just enough, at just the right time, to send me over the edge. Not that I would have admitted standing on or even close to any edge, whatsoever.

The apartment wasn't ready, that was all. Well, that wasn't all, was it? We were tired, we'd had no dinner, I'd run into a coffin in a church, it was seven o'clock, five months ago today Mike died, and the Paolo who finally emerged from behind the blue gate of the B and B (which was certainly near sea water but in no way actually on a beach), unlike the "Paolo" who wrote me friendly, chatty e-mails in perfect English, spoke no English at all and then led us to another, temporary apartment two blocks away that was bare, scruffy, had no fans, and had only enough linens for half of the three beds in it.

After that, after a walk down to the cove where we were essentially ignored in one restaurant and then served deeply mediocre pizza after another long wait at the next, after not getting back from that dreary adventure in local cuisine until after ten, they're asleep, and here I am, upset, hot, angry, frustrated, and near tears.

I had been batting a thousand, everything had gone so well, and now this miserable day happened, this July 3. I look at websites for hotels in neighboring towns (for there are no hotels here in Cava d'Aliga). I toy with just booking it out of Sicily and going to Barcelona early. We could even backtrack and return to the farm. I think I remember Claudia telling me there would be no more guests until next week. We could just go back there.

Here it is, that bottom line: I just don't want to be here, in this place, in this situation. I just want to be somewhere cleaner, where I feel as if someone kind of, sort of, gives a damn about me and can communicate such to me, where I can sleep on top of and under sheets and don't have to set aside two hours of my life to find dinner.

Where I am right now? Not where I want to be, that's all I know. I don't want to be where I am.

The walls in this place are almost bare, which doesn't help the atmosphere. What little is up there is randomly scattered, askew, and all religious, which does. Help, that is. A picture of John Paul II in the front room where the boys are sleeping in a pull-out and I'm sitting on a twin bed under the open window, a San Damiano cross in the bedroom where Katie's sleeping. Padre Pio in the kitchen. They're all here. Always, wherever I go, it seems.

I close the browser windows where I've been searching TripAdvisor and Alitalia and shut the computer. I finger what's hanging on a chain around my neck—the heart Michael gave me on our fifth anniversary, both of our wedding rings, and the crucifix he always wore, that he was wearing the day he dropped off the treadmill five months ago today.

At the hour of my death, call me.

Joseph and Michael sprawl on the large bed on the other end of the room, breathing softly. Adults fixate on what's missing here, what could be better, but for my sons, all a new place and a new apartment mean is another adventure. They were just excited opening and closing cabinet and closet doors, exploring the kitchen and bathrooms and the cool sliding door that leads to the courtyard, and talking about the beach as they would be if we were staying at the Breakers.

From my narrow bed shoved next to the low open window,

I can hear laughter down the street, from people in other apartments, other rooms, people who are happy to be here. Beyond the laughter, I can hear something else, a steady, gentle rush, receding and advancing. I settle down and try to sleep on the bare bed in the hot room. We could stay or we could go. But first, tomorrow, we'll go to the beach.

~

The next morning, Saturday morning, I'm still toying with getaway plans, but I'll wait to follow through on any of them until we experience breakfast and see the new apartment Paolo has for us. It's a sunny morning, and I can see the way to the beach down the road, so it's already better.

Katie sleeps on, so the boys and I make the interesting descent to breakfast, which takes us through the large blue wooden door to the house, down dark steps, past guest rooms, most with open doors and hung with damp towels, past what I suppose is the front desk, and then out onto a patio on the back of the house, on the hill. The sea is down there even farther, but it is mostly hidden from us and is also apparently out of bounds because of some sort of dangerous situation requiring repairmen who start to trickle through during breakfast. So yes, that part was true: there is a beach associated with the place. Not that we can actually get to it from this spot, but it's down there.

As in the photos, white tables are indeed scattered here under the trees, and other guests are sitting at them. Paolo greets us. He's effusive, already sweating, still apologizing, promising better things ahead (I gather), showing me the pastries, recommending those filled with local ricotta in particular, noting our preference for *freddo* milk.

Elena, his wife, has a broad, cherubic face and is, appropriately, always beaming, cherubically. She wears large loopy earrings, her dark curly hair is pushed back by a wide headband, and she is also very happy to see us, fluttering in and out, refilling coffees, clearing tables, her loose, caftan-type top cut so low and wide, with apparently nothing underneath it, that she seems in perpetual danger of just flying loose in a way that makes me nervous. She's delightful—well, they both are, but she also speaks no English, so the mystery remains, and I consider it while I appreciate the ricotta pastry, wipe chocolate from Michael's mouth, and pour milk (freddo) over their cereal. So who was answering my e-mails, exactly?

Well then, down the steps, Madame makes her entrance. *Buongiorno, Madame!*

Madame is in her early seventies, walks regally among the tables in a flowing caftan, nodding her head to the greetings from guests, her eyes hidden behind huge sunglasses and black hair fashioned in the same round bouffant it's been in since 1968. She's French, but when she greets me—it's *Good morning* and *We're so sorry about the confusion.*

Well, there you go. Why the e-mails didn't just come from her instead of Paolo, I don't know, especially since, it turns out she, along with her husband, *il Professore* (whom I will not meet until tomorrow), is actually the owner of this place, which Paolo and Elena manage, along with a small hotel in Donnalucata, just west of here.

Madame speaks briefly to us, tells me that she used to teach English in Paris, and indicates that Paolo has told her that we are Catholics and would like to go to Mass tomorrow. She says that the parish offers an outdoor Mass nearby for the tourist season, and she will happily call and find out the details for us.

When she says *You are Catholics*, her tone suggests that this is something exotic and strange, to be a Catholic actually interested in going to Mass, even here in Italy. Perhaps that's it and perhaps it isn't, but also it might be that we're odd in general—an American woman traveling alone with three children in southeastern Sicily—and being practicing Catholics simply adds to the curiosity factor.

I'm feeling that curiosity now, eating breakfast down here with the Italians—mostly northern Italians, I would come to understand—small family groups, some couples. Some are clearly regular, yearly visitors who know each other, know Paolo and Elena well.

A little boy eats a bit, races around the tables, then returns to his family for a few more bites, as any little boy on vacation within earshot of the sea would do.

His name is Giacomo and immediately, of course, he and Michael hit it off, kicking a ball between them and running about. Joseph joins in, too, but at his own pace, cautiously.

"Giacomo" is far too complicated for Michael, and so his new friend gets a new name: "Jack-a-boy" in Michaelspeak.

After a few minutes, Jackaboy's mother approaches my table. In her early forties perhaps, thin, with a wide gap-toothed grin and a face framed by a halo of dark curly, unkempt-on-vacation hair, she communicates to me that she knows a bit of English. She took it in school—"scholastic"—she says.

Well, she really doesn't know much English at all, as it turns out, but we manage to exchange information nonetheless, trading children's ages, where we're from (they're from Milan), and she points me toward the beach—just a couple of hundred meters down the road, an easy walk, and very nice, she says.

She's so proud of herself for coming to talk to me. She holds up her arms like a bodybuilder and declares to the breakfast group, "I am cou-rah-gous!" She's charming and I like her a lot. Her name is Domenica, and I can't help but think . . . *Buona Domenica!*

It turns out there's another, fluent English speaker at another table, a sleek-looking professional fellow in his thirties, whom Paolo rounds up to help him tell me when our new room will be ready—he's willing but, I can tell, ultimately indifferent to us and any future translation needs we might have. He lets me know that Paolo says to be ready for the big move in thirty minutes, tucks his hardbound and very biblical-looking guidebook to *Sicilia* under his arm, and heads upstairs and out for the rest of his day.

～

Our new apartment is mostly better than the last. It's closer to the B and B itself, there are four beds, although only two of them are made. It's bigger. There's a fan, which gives us momentary hope, which we lose when we discover that it requires an adaptor, and we can't find one.

The kitchen, though, is fairly grungy and the bathroom is dreadful—so bad that when I go out later, I look for a new bathmat to replace the scary one that's in there now. Well, you get what you pay for, and you get what you don't find reviews for in this travel world. It's only for a few days, I remind myself and everyone else. And, you know, I keep saying to the game but, I can tell, still very doubtful Katie—*it's the beach! Everything's scruffy and worn at the beach!*

And being a rather scruffy and ramshackle person myself, I shouldn't mind too much. But that bathroom? Not good.

Paolo brought his van to move our things—not that it was very far, and not that we couldn't have walked the two blocks ourselves, but he clearly felt we were owed. During the transition, I learned—again through our limited shared vocabulary and hand motions—that he had, in his former life, been a hairdresser—had owned salons in Milan, and I got the impression that he was, as they say, sort of a big deal. I have no idea whether or not that's true. He told me he spent some time in New York City, as well.

He is a very happy guy and I toy with asking him to do something with this hair.

～

This beach is different from all the others I've seen the past two weeks, and in good ways. It's not sea-to-street rented chairs. It's wider and more relaxed. And gone are the massage, purse, and jewelry peddlers. It's just sand and water, the town of Cava d'Aliga tumbling down to our left, the coast stretching out toward the west on the other side.

Over the next four days—we fly to Barcelona on Wednesday—we'll spend a lot of time here. We'll find time for side trips, too, but the beach will always be waiting for us. I love watching the families here, of which everyone seems to be a part, at least two generations, usually three: a father calms his squabbling children by saying, "Scusi, scusi," softly to them and then breaking into song. Old men stroll up and down the beach in their skimpy suits and loose shirts—here, as in the north, the older the man, the less cloth used for his bathing suit—strolling, talking, nodding, always with their hands clasped behind their backs. They study the sky.

An older man hears me speaking to my children and stops me. We have a very interesting conversation—he is happy to hear that I am from Alabama, for it is near New Orleans, which was a focus of his work for many years when he worked on container-ships. Flour from New Orleans to Japan, cars back from Japan to New Orleans.

When he tells me this, he struggles for the word for what traveled from New Orleans to Japan, and—the word he tentatively settles on is *green*—he has confused three words—*green, flower,* and *flour*—all at once.

Then he strikes a rather tragic pose and shakes his head. He would like to return to New Orleans, someday.

"I have not been back," he says, touching my arm and shaking his head, "since—the *tragedy.*"

I nod my head, too.

"Ah, si, Katrina," I say.

Tragedia.

In the car, after our beach time, when we're driving around trying to figure out the food situation, Katie is gradually and painfully realizing that she might have had too much sun without enough protection, and then a fight breaks out. I have no idea what it's about, but this time, all three are in it, and that's all it takes for the scale to tip in the other direction, and this time, I lose it.

I threaten to call Delta and change our flights—we can go back home tomorrow, I declare.

I halfway mean it—I more than halfway mean it. I'd already done the research, after all.

But it's also partly a test. A test to see if they are really liking this or if it is really nothing but my own self-indulgence at play here, and I'm just dragging them along, unwillingly.

The bickering ends abruptly, and after a shocked silence, the wailing begins.

"No! We don't want to go!"

"We're sorry!"

"Sorry, Mom."

"Really? You really want to stay?"

You want to stay, I'm thinking. *Really? In the grungy apartment, hot, uncomfortable, no TV, not home, alone with me in this land of friendly, yet definitely Italian Italians?* I'm honestly stunned at their passion.

"Yes! Please! We're sorry! We like it! It's fun!"

Well, now. Imagine that.

But what about me? What do I want? Right now, what do I really want?

I want—I want things to be different, that's all. It could be here, it could be anywhere. Just different. I want to have good food to eat that will be served to me without waiting for an hour, and a better apartment and I want better Internet. Well, that's superficial. And I want Mike. Sometimes that might seem superficial, to the supersaintly, heaven centered among us. But nonetheless I want him in the front seat, looking back at them sternly, then hiding a grin when he turns back around and quickly glances at me. I want those wordless glances when we know we're just thinking the same things about this funny crew.

Well, that's not happening. So I might as well stay and see what is, instead.

~

A couple of hours later, what's happening is a big Saturday night in Cava d'Aliga, population maybe a couple of thousand.

I'd noticed the preparations in the town square, high on the hill on the other side of the cove from our apartment after that earlier stormy drive. I'd dropped the kids off at the apartment, then I'd gone out by myself to do a serious, undistracted search for food, an ATM, and somewhere to buy more Internet time. Driving around the village, I noticed the piazza in front of the church, and how they were setting up a stage, testing a sound system, and unfolding chairs there.

In the early evening, I take the boys over, because Katie is suffering from her sunburn. We walk along the cove to a point at which we can take some steps, then go through a tunnel cut through a thick wall up to the center of the village. On the way, we pass a sailboat of sorts that has been parked near that tunnel— it's a sculpture, really, and it's evidently time for it to be painted. Typically, a small group has gathered around the artist wielding the brush, men with hands folded behind their backs watching, other men and women clustered closer to him, within his hearing, pointing and giving him advice. I can't tell if he's listening or not.

Once we arrive at the small piazza and I see the musicians getting ready, the craftspeople, and the food, I take them back to the apartment, get the car, and I (basically) force (poor) Katie into it, assuring her that what I was taking her to see was so unique and charming, it would be a shame for her to miss it. What was a shame was a mother making her sun-poisoned daughter leave her bed so she could watch Sicilians do jujitsu. On the Fourth of July, yes, but still.

We park across from the church, across from a statue of Padre Pio, of course, and we walk to the square.

Craftspeople sell their goods—lots of embroidery, some painting, a sandstone carver, who has some fine small tiles with crosses on them, and crosses themselves, including one with an image of Padre Pio embedded in it. It struck me as too heavy for transport at the time, but now, I can't believe I didn't buy it.

A man and two young boys are selling fried cakes—donuts of a sort, some plain, others filled. We buy three, and the boys very carefully and proudly take our money and package our sweets.

The village gathers slowly—old women first, taking their places near the front and at the sides. Then younger women and children, with men here and there, skirting the edges of the crowd. A sleek, graying, quite prosperous-looking fellow appears and is approached by many, who pay him obeisance—modern, casual obeisance, but obeisance and honor nonetheless. He seems to be more than the mayor, but who, I can't imagine, and although I am dying to know, unlike Domenica, I don't have the *cour-ahge* to inquire right now.

As night falls, the performances begin, there on the night of July fourth in the little village square of Cava d'Aliga. Children get up on stage and sing. There's the jujitsu demonstration, offered by young people in impressive black robes, who are announced by name: *Giovanni . . . Francesco . . . Giuseppi . . .* accompanied by vaguely Asian tinkling from the keyboard.

I want to do that, Joseph murmurs, and into the file it goes for future reference. If he's interested in it, if he can direct his passion, his busy mind, and yes, even his anger, he can do it.

As we leave, Solid Gold dancers of a sort are getting ready to go on, the girls in black pants and gold fringed tops with one sleeve and one bare shoulder, the boys, absurdly slim in black pants and ties, emerging confidently from a backstreet like the Jets or the Sharks, ready to rumble.

We drive back to the apartment, and once there, it doesn't take long for sun-drenched boys to fall asleep, although it takes much longer for the miserable, hurting sun-doused girl.

⁓

Earlier in the afternoon at the beach, before the backseat brawl, before the village festival, I went out into the sea.

I realized when I got out there that I could talk to him there, aloud, and no one would see me because the beach was practically empty now, and no one could hear me.

So I talked to him. I shouted because I was so, so angry with him for dying.

I cursed it all and I plunged in, and then I felt badly about it, but not really because I *was* angry with him, angry that he didn't go to the doctor for some months before, even though, even though . . . they all say, they probably couldn't have detected a thing.

I dove in again and forced myself through the water and cut through it and let it carry me and I remembered all of our times at beaches, watching and laughing, wrapped up together in the sea.

I didn't want to be in Cava d'Aliga anymore, especially, but I did want to stay in that water right there and yell at Michael and cry and beg for none of it to have happened. I was just so tired. So tired of dealing with all the children by myself, of having to make every decision on my own, of their future, it seemed, in my hands, and with not a soul to really help and not a one to bitch to.

But I had to go back. I couldn't stay out there in the water by myself. There wasn't any solace out there anyway, no assurance in the vastness of sea and sky that God is watching and taking care of us and everything will be great.

I didn't want to go back. I wanted to be alone with Michael, forever, even though I was furious at him.

I understood something then. I understood how people in this situation just give up and die, how they leave it all behind to follow.

I wasn't tempted, but I understood. I glimpsed a faint hint of how someone could just not want to be where they were anymore, how they would want to just leave, to follow what—who—has been lost . . . wherever.

The tug on that string was unmistakable, and I was glad to feel it, for I'm always glad to understand life—even the darkness in it—a little more.

But it wasn't that strong of a tug, after all, since all it took to break it was the sound of a little boy back on the shore, laughing.

~

At the end of this long day, a day of being pushed and pulled, of yearning to be anywhere else but here, everyone's asleep, the sea splashes in the distance, and I'm writing on the little front porch, thinking about the pull of the mystery of that ocean depth and an unreachable horizon. But the yearning is fading, oddly satisfied by this unexpected evening. Life was still happening, and it was as charming and joyous as villagers gathering in the square on a Saturday night to chat, to greet each other under the stars, to watch their children sing and dance and carve graceful slices from the air. The world seems bigger tonight, greater than my own tragedia, real or imagined, and I'm entranced, nostalgic, worried, tired, guilty, envious, comforted, hesitant, and hopeful all at once. I'm poised here, listening, watching, and waiting. I'm waiting right here in this place for now, waiting for Sunday. Waiting for the next day, the day of resurrection.

22

A T BREAKFAST ON SUNDAY, I AM TRYING TO CONVINCE *il Professore* and Domenica that earlier this morning, I had heard a horse.

Il Professore, the husband of Madame, is quite large and old, perhaps in his early eighties, and bald, with age spots dotting his dome. Leaning on his cane, he seems to be in continual danger of toppling over, especially as he tilts a good ear in my direction.

A retired surgeon who had spent a year or so at Johns Hopkins decades ago, he speaks some English but also admits he has forgotten most of it. He is courtly and frankly curious about how we come to be here. I make vague statements about this, claiming that we just wanted to travel off the beaten path. That I'd heard about the wonderful beaches in southeastern Sicily. I don't mention *mi sposo, morto*. I don't know why, but in this group, at this point, I'm keeping that information to myself.

As *il Professore* descended to the patio that morning, all the guests stood and greeted him reverentially: *Buona Domenica, Professore . . . Buongiorno, Professore . . . Salute, Professore.* I watched them and remembered that sharp, mysterious dignitary from last night in the square. I think of bishops and their titles and episcopal rings in a different context from egalitarian America—this one—and it fits.

But I digress. So about that horse. In those early hours of the morning, I was awakened, I'm certain, by the *clop-clop-clopping* of a horse and the clattering of cart wheels. The noise, and the possibility that I might not be dreaming it, didn't register quickly enough for me to get the shades up and check for sure, by which point, the noisemaker had traveled too far down the block for me to be able to make out what it was without my contacts in.

I assumed he (or she) was selling something, for while the beaches here are free of vendors, the streets aren't. They drive trucks full of vegetables and fruits, bumping over the cobbled and roughly paved roads, calling out through their megaphones. The mattress salesman drives around every day, plastic-wrapped mattresses fitted like Jenga pieces in the back of his truck. Cheerful music blares from a speaker mounted on the cab. This is the tourist end of town, and all I can guess is that the market here is for visitors who find they've got more people than beds for the week.

So I'm trying to explain, and since the most proficient English speaker isn't present, I struggle. I insist that I'd heard a horse cart. Domenica and *il Professore* squint at me, look at each other, and shake their heads as I keep talking and gesturing. *Aah* . . . they look at each other again, speak some Italian, and this time, they nod. *Il Professore* inquires.

"You want to go horseback riding? Yes?"

I say no, not at all, but it doesn't matter because the always enthusiastic Paolo, coffeepot in hand, has now been involved. He's delighted to help, contemplates the problem, looks into the distance as if searching for a sign, and then says, very decisively, "Pozzallo!" There are, *il Professore* translates, stables in Pozzallo, a few kilometers to the east. If I wait, Paolo can go search out the brochure he is certain he has.

Well, no but *grazie* anyway, and everyone drifts back to their tables, wondering, I've no doubt, why this woman came from America to the beach town in Sicily with the hope of finding a horse to ride and why, just when the solution was offered, she changed her mind.

Of course, once the idea of horseback riding has been raised, even unintentionally, both boys—Michael eating his apricot-filled pastry, his hair blonder than when we arrived ten days ago, I'm certain of it, and Joseph with his cereal and both with large cups of cold milk—perk up at the possibility.

Can *we go horseback riding?*

Please?

~

It's a lovely day for the beach, so we go there shortly after breakfast, and not on horses. Even Katie ventures out and sits in the chair, wrapped in a towel with a huge hat on her head, reading. I call her Aunt Catherine, which she can laugh about because she is, indeed, feeling a bit better. By midafternoon, we've had enough sun, so I suggest a little trip. We'll go to Scicli, one of the many reportedly interesting towns rebuilt after a terrible earthquake in 1693 in southeastern Sicily that killed, it's estimated, a hundred thousand people and brought everything crashing down and even split some towns in two.

At the time, the Spanish still owned Sicily, but they left the island's control in the hands of the local aristocracy. This meant that rebuilding could happen very fast—which it did—and in very grand style—which it did. The style even has its own name: Sicilian baroque—and this is one of the reasons people come to this corner of Sicily—besides the beaches and the ceramics and chocolate—to see the evidence of this fascinating outburst of creativity, born of tragedy—the palazzos, civic buildings, and churches (always churches) with their rococo details, their balconies held up by fantastical creatures and sometimes very-un-PC Moors, interiors with strong lines, nooks, crannies, and bloody, colorful statuary as big as life.

It's a short drive to Scicli, and the centro is easy to find. There's no traffic and little life about, but I'm thinking that a church or two might be open, and of course there will be gelato somewhere, I'm sure.

⤚

When Mike was alive, we had always visited churches, everywhere we went. Along with baseball and football games, museums and festivals, we'd hunt out the churches and shrines. My photographs tell the tale: four-year-old Joseph reaching to light a candle in an elaborate, layered votive holder at Saint Peter in Chains in Rome. Five- and two-year-old boys with Mike stepping out of a Russian Orthodox monastery chapel in upstate New York. Joseph in a stroller, Mike at the helm, in front of the Martyr's Church in Ontario. One-year-old Joseph crawling on the stone doorstep, preserved in a Philadelphia shrine, where St. John Neumann dropped to the ground before he died.

When we lived in northern Indiana, we took occasional trips to Detroit, either for its own sake or on the way to Canada, and every time, we visited the shrine of Father Solanus Casey. Father Solanus was a Capuchin friar who many hope will be canonized one day. Mike was one of those people and always carried a small image of him with a third-class relic pasted on the back; on one occasion, he credited the friar's intercession for saving his life on a rainy interstate west of Louisville.

Whenever Mike took his boys to Father Casey's shrine, he would tell them that they were going to see "the man in the box." And he would tell them all the stories about this Man in the Box, how he welcomed people to the friaries and prayed for them, how he served the poor, how he'd lived in our part of Indiana for a while, how he played the violin, and how he had a big beard. And we would all kneel and pray for a bit at the coffin that was raised aboveground, and Mike would make *such* a big deal about the Man in the Box. He did it in his usual way—jocular, underlined with absolute seriousness—telling the boys that the Man in the Box was really still alive with God. We could ask him for help anywhere, but especially here where his body lay. We could light candles, scribble our petitions on paper and lay them on his wooden coffin, whisper our needs and the needs of those we love, and the Man in the Box would do what he could to help us, because he lives in Love now, and love never dies.

~

I find an open church at the end of a side street off one of the piazzas. The exterior is a harmonious baroque façade: half columns and statues of saints and angels dotting two levels of beige and yellowish stucco.

We step inside the open door and nod at a middle-aged, small, bald man seated at a table near the entrance. The table is bare but for his Sprite bottle, and there are no racks of postcards or pamphlets around that he's selling. I take him to be the one charged with protecting the church against vandals and thieves on this Sunday afternoon. We nod at each other, and then he stands up, takes his Sprite, and walks deeper into the church. Our eyes adjust to the darkness, and we start to look around.

What we notice right away is the statuary placed around the church, along the aisles, in the side chapels, high above the side altars. It's full out, colorful, dramatic, and bloody. The boys love it.

Near the entrance stands one of the bloodier *ecce homos* I've seen. Jesus stands on a pedestal above us, his head bowed. His white loincloth trimmed in gold is clean as befitting a king, but his skin is broken at the chest and the knees. He's beaten and scraped, and blood is dripping everywhere.

Across the aisle, it's Jesus again, and he's stumbling. The cross is balanced on his shoulder, that arm upraised, the other hand resting on a rock, as if he is steadying himself. Two men—one leading with a rope looped around Jesus's neck, the other standing to the side, holding the Virgin back, wear knotted turbans and tights. Mary Magdalene—you will always know her because she always wears red—kneels, pleading.

These figures and the others around us with their nut-brown

skin all look at and beyond us with eyes wide in sorrow and fear. The paint on the walls around them, around us, is patched and discolored, light blues and yellows. Plants and candles are scattered at the feet of the Christ and his saints; framed pictures are propped against columns with peeling paint and chipped stucco.

Another group posed behind glass high above a side altar interests me, so I lead Katie and the boys over there to look at it. A half-naked figure—who else could it be but the dead Christ?— lies flat in the midst of a group of three other figures wearing gold-lined black robes. Some of them reach up to heaven, begging; others reach down to us below and point to the one lying there.

Look, they seem to be saying, what you've done.

On a lighter note, consider the frilly hearts!

That's what the boys are looking at and asking about: the dozens of hearts, ribbons, and lacy doilies they see tacked on the walls across from this side altar, pink on one side, blue on the other. I start to explain that these are *ex votos* that people bring when their prayers for babies have been answered. This interests the boys for only as long as it takes them to notice the votive candles, which evidently are demanding to be lit.

I'm digging for euro coins, because of course we'll light candles and we'll pray, when I spy the man from the front of the church. He's standing about fifty feet away from us, on the other side of this altar. The boys are chattering, waiting for coins for the candles; Katie is standing next to the baby hearts and flowers, looking above the altar, up at the black-robed figures pointing us to the dead Christ, just in case we think we can forget.

I see his face over there in the shadows. He is grinning and I think nothing of it for the first second; I think that he is just watching us, and that he will probably be approaching me for a handout soon. But in the next second, the grin speaks to me of something else and I freeze. I can't move, and my blood, my heartbeat, my nerves all seem to just seize up as I see what's really going on.

For the grin is no such thing. That's really a grimace on his face as he's watching the boys and the girl, surrounded by pink and blue hearts, blood and death, and he's got his pants open, his hand working vigorously, and his eyes meet mine.

~

The boys never know what happened, why we race out of the church so suddenly, and although I hoped Katie wouldn't either, I wasn't fast enough, and she saw. *She saw.*

Because of the boys, we can't talk too freely about it now, but I let her walk close to me and whisper, enraged and horrified. I whisper back something about evil. That's what it looks like, what perversion looks like. That was it. I'm sorry we saw it, but we did. I tell her that she should be upset. Evil should do that to us: it should enrage and upset us.

For a few minutes, as long as it takes us to rush without seeming to rush from the church to the piazza and gelato, I call everything into question, about that church, about Scicli, about Sicily itself and us here. Was it worth it? Are you pleased with yourself, for bringing them over here to be plunged into *that*, even though they didn't see anything, didn't know? They could have, easily. I admit that I hear Mike's voice, too, asking me what I'm doing, taking his sons to Italy, hauling them into run-down empty churches where perverts lurk.

Well, Scicli must be redeemed. It has to be. We can't leave on this note. As we sit eating gelato at outdoor tables, I make lame attempts to cheer Katie up. I point out the shop across the road that's called Happy Days, but she is still brooding, and I don't blame her.

"I don't know what would make me feel worse," she murmurs, glancing at her brothers, "if he was doing it for—to—me"—and her eyes filled with tears as she nods at them, happily chatting at their own table oblivious to anything except gelato—"or because of them."

The gelato is cold, but that's not why she's shaking.

I think that gelato is not enough, that we need another church. *I* need another church. There's a Carmelite parish on this square. It's a smaller church than the other, well-lit, it actually has other people walking around in it, and the statuary is not bloody. It shines and smiles gently, scrubbed clean. Mary and her child tower in the sanctuary, larger than life, robed in silver. Huge scapulars swing from their outstretched hands. Mary's must be a yard long. Bright flowers are everywhere, and a small silver Padre Pio watches over a side altar. A father and young son move through the aisles, the father with his hand on his son's shoulder, talking softly and pointing.

It helps. But still, when we step back outside, the piazza, surrounded by shuttered-up shops, benches filled with middle-aged and older men, with not a woman or child in sight, the scene strikes me as no longer picturesque, but sinister, and the baroque façades seem just like that: façades.

～

Back at our apartment in early evening, darkness grows and the air cools. I walk to the corner to see what's going on in that empty lot with the tent, feeling mildly vindicated—okay, *extremely* vindicated—when I must step around a pile of horse droppings. I see that the road in front of that grassy lot has been roped off, and people are starting to gather, so it looks like this Mass under the stars really will happen, just as Madame told me it would.

It's early yet, though, too early for Mass, but enough time for the rosary. We could go over to the rosary, but since it's coming to us over loudspeakers, we don't need to, not that we could pray the rosary in Italian anyway. As the boys color and draw on a table in the apartment, as Katie reads, as I sit on the tiny front porch with my computer, we can hear them.

Ave Maria, piena di grazia, il Signore è con te.

Rolling across the tile roofs under the light blue sky, around the corner on the sandy street, the prayers come.

Santa Maria, Madre di Dio, prega per noi peccatori . . .

I'm working a bit out here, readying myself for a longer haul later tonight after Mass. I contribute to a daily devotional publication, and my five devotions are due in a couple of days. With this kind of thing, of course, you have to work way ahead, so I'm sitting here in July contemplating November. When I opened the assignment a few weeks ago, my stomach tightened as I saw that one of the dates I was given was November 16. Mike's birthday. They didn't do it on purpose. They didn't know, after all.

I sit outside on the bench on our little front porch, think about what to say about that, about anything, listening.

. . . adesso e nell'ora della nostra morte.

❧

Closer to eight, we leave our apartment, and walk around the corner to go to Mass. Wrapped in jackets, we huddle on a wooden bench under the stars with perhaps a hundred other people. A statue of Mary stands next to the altar under the tent. A priest, assisted by a deacon, celebrates. The congregation sings in that mournful, diffuse, Italian congregational style.

As we stand for our prayers, I can imagine—see—Mike standing next to me. He'd have one arm crossed over his chest, and the other resting atop it, his finger over his lips, watching, absorbing, comparing, trying not to compare, trying not to play the critic, trying to pray. He'd be filing faces and moments and gestures and accents away for future reference. He'd be . . . here.

The little boys are both pressing up against me, one on either side, and as I tend to do, I get a little annoyed with them for it. I want to push back. *Give me some space*, I think. *I need some room. Stop leaning on me so much.*

And then I'm confronted with the mirror again. I think of my own prayers, how so many—too many of them—have been so fixated, to put it bluntly, on the empty space that's actually next to me, no matter how much I try to conjure up a solid presence. Pressing up against him, pulling him back to me, trying to see him, all the time.

Give him some room. Let him go.

At Communion, Joseph leans even harder and cries a little. I do too as I try to open up and let Christ in. I am feeling so many things all at once, but mostly I am feeling weak. What a loss for them, to grow up without their father pulling a rosary out of his pocket, pointing out details in a stained-glass window, and doing it all with that particular air that took hardly anything too seriously except the things that must be taken absolutely seriously. I can try, but I'm not him. Just as it would be hard for him, if the roles were reversed. I'm not Mother of the Year, but I have my gifts, and they would miss me too. But I'm not the issue.

It's all hard enough, but I think of what happened today in Scicli and it seems impossible. Evil lurks everywhere. What am I supposed to do, I wonder, I plead. And how am I supposed to do it, alone? They need you. *You.*

~

One winter day when we were still living in Indiana—so, of course, before Mike died—I was on my hands and knees cleaning the bathroom floor, when a terrible thought came to me, overwhelmed me, and even brought tears to my eyes.

I realized that I was probably not going to be with my children when they died. I don't know why I thought that. I wasn't angry with one of them, or wishing them dead. It just popped into my head, this image of one or the other of them, old, sick, and suffering, and me not there to help.

Of course, it's always possible that one of them will predecease me, but given that I have five, the chances are that most of them, if not all, will die after I'm gone, and picturing this was almost too much to bear.

It wasn't that my ego was offended, that I believed that my specific presence was essential for a peaceful death. No, I think it was simply what a mother would feel. How can I not be there when my daughter and sons prepare for the end of those lives that began deep within my own flesh?

I thought about it some more, sprayed a spot, and kept scrubbing. Well, sorry, time and space. Nice try. You can't keep me away, I determined. It won't be any different then than now. If they need me, you bet I'll be there.

~

Do you remember the Man in the Box? I do. I thought about him the day we buried Mike. Everyone else was standing around the cars, talking and waiting to leave. I was the last one at the edge of the hole in the ground; I stood there, my hands on the smooth wood of his casket, not wanting to leave, not knowing any reason to stay, and I thought, quite suddenly, *Now* you're *the man in the box.*

It almost made me laugh (because he would), even as I was crying.

As I have thought about it since, it still strikes me as ironic and kind of funny in a sad way, but also prescient. For who knows how this all rests in the boys' subconscious, in the depths of their souls?

I am so worried about the void left by Mike's death, and I am so anxious that I teach them how to fill that void with God's loving protective presence above all. I often doubt that I can do it, especially since I feel as if I am doing it alone.

But maybe not. Maybe the Man in the Box is one way Mike helped. Helps. Through those visits, even his joking references encouraged them to see that they live, not in solitude, but in the midst of a Communion of Saints. That the Man in the Box is not gone, but lives, listens, wants to help, and they can join their hearts to him and all the rest in prayer whenever they want, wherever they are. In Christ, there's no such thing as alone.

~

The Italians sing their mournful-sounding praise in the descending darkness, and the four of us are sitting close together partly because it's chilly and partly because it's where we want to be right now. It's where I want to be. I'm confounded by the Body, grieved by the Body, fed by the Body, in the midst of the Body. Yes, this is where I am. I look over and catch Katie's eye and she smiles a little. She'll be okay. I let the boys lean against me, and I even pull them in closer. I look up, and I can sense they do, too, their little heads pressed up against me. We have a straight, clear view to the heavens tonight, here on this last Sunday away from home, this *Buona Domenica* above the restless sea.

23

ONDAY AFTERNOON IN SIRACUSA, I'M ABOUT TO hand over a few euros for some tickets. Katie is stretched out on a bench on the other side of the room, fanning herself with a brochure, and the boys are studying a vending machine nearby, probably discussing which pseudofood item I'm least likely to say no to.

I pause, not letting go of the cash quite yet. The young man behind the counter waits patiently. I consider the doorway behind him that I know leads to a passage underground. I ponder the electric lantern on the counter next to this young man, both of them ready to lead us down. This all might be very interesting, but still, I wonder if this is a good idea.

Take the children for an afternoon in a place where dead people were buried?

Really?

⁓

Little boys move in and out of different worlds. They go to school, they play a sport or two, they work on a musical instrument, or they make things. They help in the kitchen, they say their prayers, they dig holes, they listen to a story. They also tend to end up playing at being warriors of one sort or another. Mine do. Week to week, exactly what kind of warriors changes: they might be from space this week or knights the next. But whatever the specifics, the scenario is always one in which someone ends up wounded, dying, or dead. Granted, with a stupid grin on his face sprawled in the grass on the front lawn, but still.

As Halloween approaches, mummies and ghosts come up more frequently in conversation. As we move through stores or drive through neighborhoods decorated for the holiday, I try to divert their attention, to take another way, and if I can't, I watch them to see if they're making any connections. I watch to see how they react to these images, if they're going ask. Ask what? I don't know, but I wait for them to ask something, maybe about that hand reaching from under the earth in the shadow of the fake tombstone in the neighbor's yard.

But they never do. The jokes are still jokes to them, the images of death don't seem to have anything to do with what they've lived through. The fake graves, the rubber rotting corpses don't give them pause. The real thing, though, might be a different story.

〜

If we make it down there, those catacombs of San Giovanni will probably be our last stop during this Monday day trip to Siracusa. We arrive in the morning, and spend the rest of it at the Archaeological Park amid yet another array of ruins, this time with Romans added to the Greek mix. A UNESCO World Heritage Site, like the Valley of the Temples, it had its moments: the huge hollowed-out cave nicknamed "Dionysius' Ear," supposedly a former dungeon of sorts, but really probably not, a towering space in which the boys' voices—even their whispers—echo and bounce off the walls. A highlight should be the Roman amphitheater with a marvelous view to the sea, something I have really looked forward to seeing. It's a disappointment, though, because it's either being readied for a performance or recovering from one. We stand between tech booths at the rim looking down over the semicircle on the side of the hill. The stone seating spread below us is completely covered with new plastic seat forms—with backs, even—and wooden platforms cover any remnants of the ancient stage.

In the early afternoon, we walk the kilometer or so to downtown Siracusa, window-shop, find some pizza and eat it. We then search for and find the shrine I'm looking for, which is not very challenging since it towers over Siracusa, its enormous sweeping cement roof looking as if a giantess's pleated prom dress had been dropped in the middle of town. The shrine is Madonna delle Lacrime—Our Lady of the Tears—and the suggestive name naturally prompts questions:

"Why is Mary crying?"

I resist the temptation to say that she's probably crying because they gave her such an ugly church and instead read them the real story from a brochure. In 1953, for three days a plaque of Mary on a Siracusan woman's bedroom wall wept. The event was filmed, the tears were tested and found to possess the qualities of human tears, and eventually the local bishop declared the event to have been authentic. *The reality of the lachrymation cannot be put into doubt*, they said. In 1994, Pope John Paul II was here to dedicate the shrine.

> *They are tears of prayer: the Mother's prayer that gives*
> *strength to every other prayer, and that rises in supplication*
> *for all those who do not pray because they are distracted by a*
> *thousand other interests, or because they are obstinately closed*
> *to God's call.*

"Did it really happen?" Joseph asks, and I am struck by the implications of his question, implications that he doesn't even grasp. He's innocently asking *did it really happen*, not understanding that *no* would mean he was walking around in a lie.

Did it really happen? I ask it all the time, not about Mary's tears, but about that loving Creator God, about Jesus risen from the dead. My own problem is not grasping the implications of *no*, but rather, embracing the consequences of *yes*.

The image that wept is here. It's encased in glass, hanging on a white marble wall behind the main altar. Katie takes the boys up to light candles, and, quite predictably, I can see from back here in the pew, a squabble breaks out up there, probably about who gets to light what, Michael insisting that, yes, he is big enough to hold the flame himself.

A father and son rise from a pew in front of me and go stand in front of the image. The father talks softly to the boy, and they fold their hands. Cross themselves.

The candles are lit, and my children come sit next to me. Joseph, of course, presses his body next to me and begins to cry a little.

All at once, I'm angry. I don't often get angry, and I never get angry for my own sake, but always for theirs. The consequences of *Yes, God loves us and Christ the Lord redeems us* are great for Mike, and they will be great for us someday, too. But what about now?

What's the point of these tears?

~

Before I can stand there thinking about the wisdom of the catacombs, I must first get some cash to pay for the possible tickets, so while Katie and Michael wait in the reception area, Joseph and I walk in a light drizzle, to try to find an ATM.

We walk past the gentle stony façade of the church that collapsed in the 1693 earthquake, but was never rebuilt, past the playground in front of it, down the street.

Joseph asks me, "What happened to the bodies of the people who died?"

It takes me a minute, but I eventually see that he's a little worried. He thinks that when he goes down into the catacombs, he'll see bodies, skeletons lain out on shelves, because he already knows that's where the dead were laid to rest.

I tell him that oh, no, there won't be any bodies. They're long gone.

"Where did they go?"

I explain. Dust to dust.

"Is that what happens to Daddy?"

I breathe in, pray for a little help here, and tell him that God makes us new bodies in heaven. Our bodies, but new. Not as if I expect him to understand, for I don't. But I give it a shot.

Joseph's words ring in my head as I put my card in the machine and wait for the cash.

Is that what happens to Daddy?

He disintegrates?

Disappears?

Gone?

Is that it?

❧

Over the course of the school year, that year that Mike died, Joseph took a little Latin class.

They met after school, it was informal and small with a conversational bent, and he learned some things. At the end of the year, they had a party. There were snacks and a demonstration class in which the children showed off their learning—they sang, they conjugated, they counted.

The children received certificates, too, and as the teacher presented them, she asked each child about their family members who were present. She would ask where they were, and the child would point, indicating they understood the Latin.

Ubi est mater?

Point.

Ubi est soror?

Point.

It was finally Joseph's turn. He received his certificate and he was asked his question.

Ubi est frater?

A look of utter, total confusion descended and wiped the expectant smile off his face. His eyes widened, as if he were begging her.

The teacher cheerfully repeated the question.

Ubi est frater?

Now he looked as if she had reached across the room and slapped him. Even as his lips tightened into that corkscrew, that near smirk, and he started to glance at me, I understood exactly what was in his head.

He couldn't remember, he wasn't sure. *Frater?*

Father?

"*Brother*," I said, too loudly, immediately, as I realized what he was thinking. "Where is your *brother*?" I said it again, perhaps unnecessarily, perhaps hoping to wipe the memory of the moment out of his mind with my litany. "*Brother.* Where is he?"

As it happened, the brother was under a table, a grinning mouth rimmed with cookie crumbs.

But still, the question hung in the air, not the question that was asked, but the one that was heard, for it was a familiar one to us all.

Ubi est . . .

~

The tour guide for the catacombs is a slim young man in tight jeans and high-top tennis shoes, who speaks excellent, if exaggerated and very precisely articulated, English. He takes note of our languages and switches effortlessly between Italian and English for the group of about fifteen who follow him and his electric torch down into the caverns.

After he explains what we'll see down there and why we can't be just let loose to wander—in short, we'd get hopelessly lost—he leads us down. It's cool down here under the ground, the ruined church, the road, under the twenty-first century. The boys stick close to me; Katie walks ahead, to better hear our guide. We walk upright, for the space is large, and the ceilings in this space are high above us. The paths that wind between the walls where the dead were laid are about ten feet wide, the space is clean and fairly well-lit, so I don't feel claustrophobic, and it doesn't feel too gloomy or morbid.

The guide explains how the bodies were laid, how the Christian living treated them. He points out a few tombs of the wealthy. We move quietly through this place, and I murmur at Michael not to touch, and I watch Joseph move past the niches and shelves carved out from the rough stone walls, and I wonder what he's thinking as he sees that there are no bodies here, that nothing remains, that this city is empty now.

～

A week or so after the Latin class, we were walking into a grocery store after the Sunday Mass celebrating the Feast of the Ascension.

Since heaven had been the subject at hand during Mass, angels came up afterward, in the car. St. Michael was one of those angels, true, but as Michael himself pointed out, he was no angel, because he did not, after all, have wings.

As we walked through the parking lot, I spread out the keys in my hand, to which were attached a colored enamel medal of St. Michael and a tiny statue of St. Joseph, enclosed in an acrylic pyramid. I pushed St. Michael and St. Joseph next to each other on my palm, and Michael and Joseph stood there in the parking lot, studying what had been their father's key chain.

"He carried Michael and Joseph with him all the time," I pointed out.

We continued on to the store. It was after Mass, we were going to get donuts or something for them, a Diet Coke and a paper for me, and then we were going to go to the park, where they would play until it was time to go hit an open house or two. The Indiana house had seen some strong interest, and I was hopeful I might be able to buy something down here soon. It was fun to look, anyway.

Apart from the house, the words of St. Paul that I'd heard proclaimed at Mass were working their way through my system. It was just a snippet of a sentence, but it stuck with me:

that you may know what is the hope . . .

And I thought of hope, and I thought of the apostles, having seen Jesus apparently disappear from their midst, being asked by two strangers, *Why are you standing there looking up at the sky?*, as they stood there, wondering . . . *Where did he go? Ubi est?*

Ahead of me, the boys were chattering nonsense, but in the midst of it Joseph paused, stopped, and asked, "When in February was it?"

He was calm. Just sort of interested.

"When—" I stuttered.

"February what?" he persisted.

"February 3," I said, and before I could breathe back in again, almost like a period at the end of my sentence he said, "He died . . ." and nodded.

And walked on, two seconds later, back in the argument about donuts.

I don't know why he asked, and perhaps I should have inquired. But I didn't, because it seemed to be an internal, private conversation he was having, a question perhaps he couldn't even have articulated if I'd asked. And that's the way it is down here. Some days we're frozen into perplexed silence and we can't think, and other days we can.

Clouds were gathering above us, I noticed. The park might not work, and plans might have to be changed. I looked up at the sky, studied it, searched it, but I couldn't see very far; I couldn't see through the clouds. I had my hopes as to what was up there, certainly, but from where I was standing, I really couldn't tell for sure.

24

On Tuesday, I made a momentous discovery.

We'd spent a memorable two weeks here in Sicily. It was mostly great, full of new sights, scents, and tastes, and a cast of characters I hope we won't ever forget. We learned about Normans and Saracens, Greeks and Romans; we discovered volcanoes, great and small; we witnessed darkness, but we mostly enjoyed a lot of light.

But this day? I'll remember this day for a very long time, too. I really can't believe it's happened right here in a bakery in Modica. You really don't know how excited I am right now.

Today is the day I learned how to pay for parking.

⟞

I take us to Modica for our last day trip because it's only about twenty kilometers away, is famous for chocolate, and was split in two by that earthquake. Sounds like a decent day trip.

We drive around upper Modica first; I am, I'm ashamed to say, amazed. Amazed because this town is completely different from anything I've encountered in Sicily so far, which is not saying anything definitive about Sicily, but just about where we've been and what we've seen over the past two weeks. Upper Modica has an utterly contemporary vibe. There are what seem to be office and industrial parks on the outskirts, nothing run-down and abandoned as it was, say, in Aragona. The streets in the centro are wider and straighter, the traffic courses more calmly than I'm used to, and the people are younger, prosperous and professional looking. I wonder what Modica's secret is.

It takes me a while, but we eventually reach lower Modica, where the chocolate and the churches are. Parking is going to be a challenge, and I have just about given up after my tenth time up and down the main drag when a space opens up and I pull in.

But now . . . what?

There is no way that this is free—no way on earth that you would park in a busy downtown anywhere in the world and not have to pay. But again, I can see no signs; there are no meters, and there are no boxes with slots at the end of the block or anywhere else. But I really, really don't want another parking ticket, and even less do I want to be blocked or towed with a plane to catch tomorrow. There's a high-end arts and craft shop here, so I poke my head in and ask the woman if she speaks any English. She does—excellent, proficient English, and so I ask her the question that has dogged me for two weeks.

"*How* do I pay for parking?"

She tells me to go to the bakery two doors down. I tell them that I want to park and for how long. They will give me . . . something.

So this I do. No one in the bakery speaks English, but we come to a mutual understanding. The proprietor pulls a quarter sheet of paper from a stack, a paper printed with a grid of numbers—the hours of the day. He asks me how long? I guess— and to be safe I say two hours. It's around 11, so he punches out the 11 and the 12 from the sheet, tells me to put it on the dashboard of the car, and takes my euro or two.

The answer, it turns out, is not simple, is probably common in cities around the globe and not news to anyone but me, but it strikes me nonetheless as ingenious, even in its convolution.

～

We don't see much in Modica, unfortunately, since we're right up against the reposa. We take in a couple of churches and taste and buy some Modica chocolate, which is grainier and not nearly as sweet as the chocolate we're used to. We get gelato and granita.

Before we go—well before our two hours are up—we find a single open shop of Sicilian goods, particularly arranged for the tourist. The young owner speaks English well, so while the children are shopping for souvenirs for themselves and for their friends back home, I talk to him about things Sicilian, and, in the end, the reposa.

I remark on his being open, and he admits that other shopkeepers consider it unfair, but he wants to be available for the tourists. He believes in Sicily, he loves Sicily, he wants more people to come to see what he loves, but sometimes these Sicilians make it hard. But then, we both agree—if you change it to make it more convenient, is it still Sicily?

As much pain as it gives us, as confusing as it can be, if my life could be changed into what I'd like it to be, would it still be my life? Would I even recognize it?

❧

Early evening, we're on the beach, and everything around us is shaded in orange.

Katie is out swimming. She stands still in the water and watches a couple over a few dozen meters to the left of her. They stand embracing out in the deep water. She might come back and point them out, testing me to see what I think of that, assuming that I'll judge them. I won't, because there's nothing wrong with it. It's good to be intertwined, to be weightless, held up together in the water's strong embrace.

Michael is on the sand in front of me, dancing and singing.

Mommy Padre Pio, Daddy Padre Pio, Joseph Padre Pio . . . Katie Padre Pio . . .

Joseph works on a castle. He's discovered the technique of getting the sand just wet enough but not too wet so that you can hold your hand like a tube and let the wet-enough-but-not-too-wet sand drip through it and rise in peaks, like frosting, like whipped cream.

I take a photo of what he's made because it's elaborate and intricate, he's worked on it, but we can't take it with us. I also like it because it evokes Gaudí's Sagrada Família church to me, and that's where we're going next: to Barcelona.

Just after I take the photograph, another boy backs up for a soccer kick, doesn't see where he's going, and steps right on and through Joseph's masterpiece that he's worked so hard on. It's wrecked.

Joseph is saddened and angrily destroys what is left. I sit with him and convince him to start building again. I take the sand and make tubes with my own hands and drip it down beside him, building towers next to his.

I tell him that in Barcelona, there will be a church that looks like this. That maybe the man who built it did this when he was a little boy—dripped sand into fantastic shapes on the beach. And maybe when he grew up he decided he would try to build it in real life.

"What was his name?" he asks me.

"Antoni Gaudí."

"Why did he build a church?"

"Because he wanted to do it for God. Some people think he was a saint."

"Why didn't he do it in America?"

"Because he didn't live in America."

He gets an idea. He's inspired.

"Maybe I'll do it in America!" He thinks again and frowns. "Oh, no. But that would be being a copycat."

"You can do it your own way."

"I could make it a church, my own church," he says, grinning again. "I could call it Padre Pio! I could make a pancake house . . ."

Michael is in the water in front of us now, splashing and still singing.

Michael Padre Pio . . . Joseph Padre Pio . . . Daddy Padre Pio.

I ask him why he's singing that, although part of me doesn't want to know, for I am sure, like Daddy's plane, what's in his head isn't as mystical as what's in mine.

"Because it's a funny name!"

~

The three of them are out in the sea now. Katie's holding on to both of them, but I still pray. I pray *Lord Jesus, protect them*, and then I realize with a start how little I pray to God these days.

For I am still seeking Mike.

Looking for Mike everywhere, even in Sicily, and he is dead.

~

Two weeks after he died, on a Tuesday, they had a memorial Mass for Mike in the cathedral in Birmingham. I sat there through most of it thinking, *Why am I in the cathedral in Birmingham, Alabama, listening to people say nice things about Michael, who can't be, but apparently is, dead?*

The bishop preached a homily that was substantive, scripture centered, focused, and, I might dare to say, charming because in that homily he gave his friend Mike due and affectionate credit for keeping him on track, always reminding him to keep his preaching substantive, scripture centered, and focused. He referred to the Gospel reading, which had related what Jesus said about Nathanael, calling him a "man without guile," and then saying, yes, that was his friend Mike.

After Mass, after the reception, a priest who had been in attendance asked to see me. He had something he needed to tell me.

He had never met either Mike or me before, although he knew of us both. Since Mike had died, he had kept us in his prayers—all sorts of prayer, he said. Offering Mass for us, rosaries, Holy Hours.

He told me he had a message for me, and that he was certain this message was from God, for it had come to him during a Holy Hour, unbidden, out of the blue.

I gripped the desk in the office, for that's where we were, and Mike's secretary was there, too. She was listening. She heard. I felt myself go weak, for this was quickly turning into a true Mike moment. Mike, who was fascinated by mysticism, who had taught discernment of spirits, who had interviewed purported visionaries on behalf of the church, who could reel off a list of his own experiences of the transparency between here and eternity.

The priest looked at me and spoke carefully.

"Tell Amy," the priest said, "that Mike is watching out for her and that he says the answer is 'yes.'"

He threw up his hands, as if to say, *And so it is. I'm just the messenger.* He repeated it. "That's the message."

The answer is yes.

But what was the question?

I pondered this, but tried not to overthink it. I tried to open myself to let the question be raised without too much input from me.

At first, I thought it was one thing—that came to me fairly quickly. That yes, he loved me, that I shouldn't doubt that. No regrets, okay?

Then some days later, I was sitting at Sunday Mass, and the second reading was proclaimed:

I swear by God's truth, there is no Yes and No about what we say to you. The Son of God, the Christ Jesus that we proclaimed among you—I mean Silvanus and Timothy and I—was never Yes and No: with him it was always Yes, and however many the promises God made, the Yes to them all is in him.

Something inside me broke open. I understood. I think I understood, for I can never be too definite about these things. But the conviction swept over me, and along with it, peace. For that moment, at least, peace.

Mike knew me, and one of the things he knew about me was my natural tendency to skepticism and my struggle with doubt. He knew that, for example, this is one of the reasons I am so affected by Pope Benedict, whose work reflects a familiarity with doubt and therefore, profound answers to it.

Lord help my unbelief.

It was sort of a joke between us—him calling me to task for my skepticism, for my overthinking. A skepticism, I'll argue, which is not a desire that these things be false or a seeking to disprove, but a yearning for definitiveness, for the experience of certainty that touches more than my intellect. A hunger, I suppose, for a full embrace of Love.

Is it real? That's all I want to know. *Is it true?*

Mike knew that this was my question. He knew me, he knew my basic, essential question, that tormented me, that held me back. He still knows. And now, where he is, he can answer it.

And he says that the answer is yes.

~

In the months since that day, I had clung to the *yes*, forgotten the *yes*, remembered it again, ignored it, and circled it, eyeing that *yes* with hope, suspicion, gratitude, and disbelief. I yearned for the firm ground of *yes*, but could not reach it because of the waves.

~

And so here we are, our last night in Sicily, at the beach. It's an almost perfect moment. Even though evening is falling, the sun is hot, but not hot enough to burn. The water has warmed up a bit.

It is one of those last few hours in a place so ideal that it makes you regret the bad things you said and thought about it and regret that it is the last day, to regret what will be lost, what opportunities you might have missed—we should have come an hour earlier, we should have spent all day here and left Modica for another time. But if we had done that, if we had spent all day here, would it still be the same as this, suffused with a relaxed orange light?

Should we have done something else? Taken another road? I don't know. I don't have those answers. I can't live in hypotheticals. The past—both real and imagined—may settle in layers around me, I may pick my way around it, but it's now I'm living in, not then.

Two boys, one brown, without a single red spot, the other burned and peeling, play joyously, one intent on battles, the other uninterested in them.

They come together. They work together. They separate. One on the castle, one on roads.

The sun is hot as it prepares to set. It's giving us one last blast. The water shimmers almost as if from within, but it's really far above. It would blind us if we tried to follow it to the source. Those in the water have no features. They are like shadows to me.

I think I want to come back just to this place, but then I think—no—there might be other places. Better. Different stories to hear and tell. Why here?

I think of travels, and then I think of home and wonder what's waiting there except absence. I wonder if I will ever feel at home anywhere again, understood, comfortable, at ease, embraced.

For that is what Mike took with him that morning. In trying to name the loss, I've settled on this. It wasn't perfectly complete because we are human and limited and because this is earth, not heaven, but it was the most home I had ever experienced, and the loss of that is starting to hit me hard. No home.

He went away and took it and left me here, yearning for home. And maybe that is the point of all of this. That in each other on earth, in love, we glimpse a bit of home, enough to ground us for just a bit, and enough to show us what home really is, what is wanting, and what is waiting.

It's time to go in the water, which is warmer today. It has not slapped me with a chill like it did before, giving me pause, making me hesitant to enter.

I can plunge right in, not alone this time, but with a boy hanging on to each hand, a girl diving in ahead of us.

So there's a reason to keep going and more, a reason to find joy, hang on to it, and bring more of it. It's not disrespectful or lacking in mindfulness. It's the opposite. It's gratitude, which at root is for God, but I can admit I need something more concrete, and they're here with me on the beach.

For what do you say to little children when they suffer a loss? Do you say, *Well, that's it. Give up and give in. I am! The rest is waiting and enduring. So sad?*

No. You wouldn't ever want your children to respond to suffering that way, to even the most profound loss, to the greatest pain. Here in the sea, I clutch their hands more tightly and let them tread in the sea, safely, and I know this. I know what I want. I want them to grow in deep sympathy and compassion as a fruit of their pain, to know how closely they are bound to others because everyone suffers, everyone is filling the hole, everyone is treading water, everyone is bubbling just under the surface that's thin and cracked and sometimes even breaks wide open.

I want them to be grateful and ecstatic and to laugh and cheer for their favorite teams and make brave choices and serve others and pray for them, to be still and know that He is God. I want them to repent and accept forgiveness, to surround themselves with the saints, and to wake up every morning, whatever place they have landed that day—whether it be familiar or strange—grateful, ready. Ready for more of this ridiculous, confusing, chaotic gift, the whispers and the shouts, the weeds and the wheat, the misty, terrifying heights, the building up and the tumbling down into ruins, the beautiful, awesome hints of what is to come, of the place where the One who loves us and who we love most— and all the others we love so much, too—calls out to us to set our sights, fiercely and with joy, knowing and trusting, unafraid to ask the questions, assured that the answer awaits.

They look up at me as we stand here on Sicilian sands, wet hair dripping, grinning, their faces that hint at their father's eyes, his grin, his passionate soul. I see those faces and I know exactly what I want for them and what grace will surely strengthen me to give.

I want them to know that the answer . . . is yes.

Epilogue

WE LIKED BARCELONA A LOT, TOO. IN FACT, KATIE loved it so much she determined she'd live there some-day, and perhaps she will.

We saw the real Sagrada Família in Barcelona, and the houses Gaudí designed and his Parc Güell, the one with the lizards clothed in bright glassy mosaic. We went to Mass in the cathedral, and afterward we watched the *sardana*, the traditional folk dance that happens there in the square every Sunday. Whoever wants to enters the circle, drops their purses and bags in the middle of the group as a sign of trust, joins hands, and begins to dance.

We learned what *valle* meant, for that is how you spell the word (the "v's" pronounced rather like "b's"), which Katie's friend Lupe repeated so often on the flight over. An English expat was entertaining a table of visiting friends in an outdoor café, and he spent a great deal of their dinner on his cell phone, speaking to someone in Spanish, saying that—*valle, valle*—over and over. That was the first thing they asked him when he finally shut the phone and turned back to them: *What does that word you kept saying—what does "valle" mean?* He told them what I'd guessed—that it's the kind of multipurpose expression that every language seems to have, that means anything from *okay* to *sure* to *Got it?*

We rode the subway and buses everywhere in Barcelona, and I was so relieved to be freed from driving for a while. The children were relieved to not be eating pastries for breakfast, and the three of them consumed a boxful of cereal and a half a gallon of (cold) milk in the first twenty-four hours of our stay. We still waited as long as the boys could stand it to eat dinner out, but we still ended up sitting awkwardly alone in restaurants, even at nine o'clock.

We watched the somewhat cheesy but still delightful light and music show put on by the enormous Magic Fountain of Montjuïc one night, we explored the impressive maritime museum down by the water, we visited the Chocolate Museum, and we even stood and cheered the Tour de France as it raced through the city one afternoon.

When we returned to the airport for our flight home, it was a bright sunny morning, and we were both sorry to end this, but also ready. We were ready to go back home, as many questions as home raised for us, as puzzling and as sad as the stillness back there still might be.

We checked our bags and we went to sit down for a while before we headed past security up to our gate. We returned to the spot where we'd rested that first blurry, exhausted morning in Europe, three weeks before: that row of chairs against the wall of windows, under the gorgeous model with the flowery, flowing dress. And he was still there.

Sleeping just where he had been when we arrived, stretched out on the seats, wrapped in a dirty coat, his head covered by a knit cap, the shopping cart stuffed with worldly goods, covered in a tarp, next to him.

We had come and gone, flown away, driven in circles, and returned. But there he was. It was as if we hadn't gone anywhere at all.

~

On February 3, the first anniversary of Mike's death, I had just closed on a new house, and I needed to meet with an electrician there. An odd way to mark the day, but what was I going to do? Every hour was marked anyway and wouldn't be denied in my head, even as I argued with myself about the arbitrary nature of "year." Why does "a year" mean anything more or less than 364 days or 366?

I don't know. But it does—or I let it. I marked the hours and remembered what I knew about those early morning hours a year ago and imagined the rest from what I had been told. Couldn't help it. Thinking about 7:30, then 8:30, and now it was 9:30, so close to the time the doctor wrote on the death certificate, which was 9:28.

The electrician spread out his papers on the kitchen island. Before he got down to telling me about breaker boxes, he moved some of my papers scattered on that counter aside, and he said something. A couple of sentences that confused me. I didn't know what he was talking about, I couldn't figure out the context.

Then I saw what he was holding. It was a Mass card sent to me by a friend for this day. The electrician had picked up this card and was admiring it.

"It's gonna be so pretty, isn't it?" he said to me.

I was still confused, thinking he was talking about my house, and wondering why.

He held the card up, showing me.

"It's gonna be *so* pretty," he repeated exactly a year after, almost to the minute. "I can't wait."

It was a little kitschy, that card. Jesus was walking on clouds, surrounded by light, walking toward an opening in more clouds, toward more light, nothing but light there. But kitsch or not, light is still light. The light that makes everything is clear, where love never ends, where there's no doubt, regret, or good-bye. I caught a glimpse. God's light.

I can't wait.

ACKNOWLEDGMENTS

In a way, this entire book is an expression of gratitude to all of the family, friends, and readers who have supported us, prayed for us, and shared their own stories of loss over the past three years.

It's also written in gratitude to the beautiful, friendly people of Sicily. Their names have been changed to protect their privacy.

In relation to the book itself, I'm grateful to Trace Murphy, who listened to my proposal and gave me the opportunity to write it. Many thanks to Gary Jansen, my editor at Image. Gary was extraordinarily patient during the year and a half we worked on this book as my rather inchoate vision took a firmer shape, in large part due to his insights. I'm grateful for Gary's help in focusing my writing, overcoming my doubts, and for making me laugh—quite often through my tears. I needed that.

Several friends read parts or all of this manuscript at various stages. I'm grateful for their comments and encouragement: Dorian Speed, Bethany McGwin, Ann Engelhart, Matthew Lickona, and David Scott.

And, of course, to Mike. You were right about a lot of things, I've discovered, and I'm grateful. Most of all, you were right about that night I drove us, Brian, and Tony all around central Florida. Remember? The night we ended up seeing Warren Zevon singing about *those heavenly mansions . . . Jesus mentioned . . .* on St. Pete Beach? That night you'd always bring up for years afterward, slyly, looking at me while I shook my head, you declaring *that was the best time . . . ever . . .*

Well, you were right about that. Because it was.

Thank you.